Michael & Me

Our Gambling Addiction
...my cry for help!

Richard Esquinas

with Dave Distel

Athletic Guidance Center Publishing
Emerald Shapery Center • 402 W. Broadway • Fourth Floor
San Diego, California 92101
(619) 595-4880

Book cover design: Chris Stell

Typesetting: Chris Stell

Photography: Essy Ghavameddini

Library of Congress Cataloging in Publications Data
Esquinas, Richard, 1955 -
Michael & Me
Includes bibliography
1. Gambling, personal narrative
2. [B] Jordan, Michael
3. Golf
I. Distel, Dave, 1944 - II. Title
HV6001-72205 E 1993   364.172   93-71766
ISBN 0-9637177-1-5

0 9 8 7 6 5 4 3 2 1

Acknowledgements

It took many people to make this project happen, probably more than we will remember to thank...

Our wives, Kerry Esquinas and Lynn Distel,
  for tolerance, support and suggestions.

Dr. Lori Stephenson, for months of insight.

Dr. Hugh Stephenson, for research and consulting.

Harry Cooper for entrepreneurial inspiration.

J. Michael Wilson, Keith Zacharin and Ed Davis,
  for legal advice.

Chris Stell, for design and type production...and patience.

David Hunt, for marketing support.

Randy Gerson, for production coordination.

Essy Ghavameddini, for photography.

Fred Sarno, Ron Heitzinger and Eric Weinberg,
  for anecdotes.

"To those in need of the
courage to reach out,
before it's too late."

Michael & Me

Table Of Contents

Chapter One

Out of Control

Statistics lie. Record books lie. I know that. I can tell you for a fact. I've seen the Official Media Guide of the PGA Tour, which has more numbers than you can possibly care to read.

I looked under the leading money winners for 1991. This statistical bible states as gospel that Corey Pavin was the leading money winner. It says he earned $979,430. That may have been enough to earn more than hackers such as Tom Kite and Tom Watson and Curtis Strange and Greg Norman and Seve Ballesteros, but none of those guys were in my league.

Not in 1991. I earned $1.25 million playing golf that year. Of course, I had an advantage over those guys.

I didn't have to tee off in the misty hours of a Thursday morning with 150 guys, any one of whom was as likely to shoot six-under-par as six-over-par, maybe more likely. I didn't play in tournaments with monster galleries, television cameras and Vin Scully talking in hushed tones from an ivory tower over the 18th green.

My tournament field was very small. I made all my money playing against one other guy, and he sometimes had trouble breaking 80.

We played for incredible amounts of money. Our money. No sponsor was throwing in the cash to get its logo into

America's living rooms. Our matches frequently came down to $100,000 putts with occasional swings of upwards of a quarter-million dollars. To put this in perspective, the difference between winning and finishing second in a million dollar PGA tournament is a mere 72 grand.

Two of us went at it like this, coast-to-coast, mano-a-mano, for more than 2,000 holes of golf, most of it in daily 36-hole chunks.

Just me and Michael Jordan.

———

This is my story. I have gambled since I learned to play craps from a neighborhood kid in one of the worst areas of Columbus, Ohio. I gambled on hoops in college, where I once took out a "student loan" to pay off a bookie. I have played cards for stupid amounts. And I make an annual Super Bowl wager of $2,500 to $5,000.

Most of all, I gamble on my own golf game. I could make $100,000 matches with a telephone call. I have had people offer to back me in six-digit matches. However, I always preferred to stay with my regular buddies and play for sensible amounts of money.

I did not get totally wild—let's call it out of control— until I encountered an opponent who had the financial where- withal to bet outlandish amounts and the athletic renown to make such encounters stimulating and challenging. The money alone was not enough of a rush. The adversary had to be worthy.

Michael Jordan was a most worthy adversary. And I was a worthy adversary for Michael. I was and still am an owner of the San Diego Sports Arena. I ran the place when we first met. I have a long and successful business history. My financial and personal background was thoroughly investigated before the San Diego City Council approved my partner and I as the new lease owners of the arena in 1989. M.J. could be confident I wasn't peddling cocaine or even beating my dog.

I don't know if he considered that someday I might write a book about our adventures.

Probably not.

I have spent countless hours soul-searching and debating within my head about whether to write this book. The potential repercussions, both for myself and for Michael Jordan, are immense.

I decided it was the right thing to do. It was right for my recovery from my addiction to gambling and the right way to reach out to a friend I perceived had the same problem. And it was a right way to heighten the country's awareness of a cancerous compulsion.

Gambling in the United States is like a train track running through a largely-unconcerned neighborhood. A few folks issue stern warnings about the potential for danger, but there is not enough of a groundswell to get anything done.

One day, almost predictably, tragedy strikes and everyone is appalled that nothing had been done, that no one could see it coming.

This is my effort at throwing myself on the tracks in front of that oncoming train. This is my effort at showcasing a problem. Compulsive gambling has grown by leaps and bounds in the U.S. for hundreds of thousands of men and women, most of whom deny it. Gambling, as an addiction, is so much more easily deniable than alcoholism or drug abuse. I lie there on the tracks struggling with my own tendency to deny.

Michael Jordan is right there with me on those tracks, whether he likes it or not.

My life has been one gamble after another, though many of the risks I have taken would not come under gambling as purely defined. I have swashbuckled from a most modest childhood to a fast track life in the worlds of entertainment and sports.

Personally, I felt I was a controlled gambler until Michael and I went berserk in one period of approximately 10 days in September of 1991, when I went from potentially more than $200,000 in debt to $1.25 million ahead. If a swing of almost $1.5 million on "games" of golf is not out of control, I can't imagine what is.

███

Neither Michael nor I are lesser human beings because of our binge, which was actually the culmination of four summers in which we danced on the edge of insanity.

What we were doing was not illegal. Just stupid. Risk comes with revelation, however, both to Michael and me.

I face potential harm to the reputation I have built as a successful business executive. This could impact my potential for future earnings far greater than would be compensated by any revenue generated by this book. I face dealing with the perception, which is far from reality, that I will dump duties for a good golf bet.

I also understand my disclosure of our adventure could have a negative impact on Michael. Those closest to him are surely aware that he has this problem with gambling, but I am not sure if his many sponsors have any idea of its magnitude. The National Basketball Association must be wary because of previous incidents at a much lower level of risk, albeit they reportedly involved rather unsavory characters.

Another consideration was that I would lay myself open to scrutiny and criticism for merely opening the shades to let the world get a peek at the mess one of its icons got into with a little-known but successful business executive. The bottom line is that I am not squealing *on* M.J., but rather telling a story *about* the two of us.

In truth, I hope I give Michael a look at the Michael he doesn't see. I may be the only person who fully understands his problem, because I have the same problem. I also hope others with this same problem will see themselves and recognize what is really there.

How else to accomplish this?

———

I sought help. I went to a therapist in November of 1991 and I continue working with the therapist and a consultant. I read extensively on gambling. I attend Gamblers Anonymous meetings.

When I first called the La Jolla office of a clinical psychologist, to make an appointment, I just told her I had some stuff I wanted to discuss. I wasn't specific, because the gambling was just part of it and I didn't really see it as a problem.

Part way through our first session, I casually mentioned the gambling I had done with a famous sports figure the previous summer. I was totally nonchalant.

She wanted to know the kind of numbers I was talking about.

I told her and I could see the shock register on her face. She was expecting I might say something like a hundred grand. She had never heard of gambling at our level.

She felt I was out of control.

I was aghast. Me, Richard Esquinas, out of control? No way. I didn't agree with her at all. I wouldn't believe I was out of control, so M.J. could hardly have been out of control. He was the one who kept pushing the wagers upward, so I assumed a million-dollar loss would be quite manageable for him.

She kept saying we had a problem, and I kept defending both of us. I'm talking now over a succession of sessions. She kept pressing the issue of payment, reminding me that I had yet to see any of the money I had won.

There is no blueprint for the best way to either understand or handle this gambling compulsion, especially when dealing with a man of M.J.'s immense popularity.

Obviously, I cannot flat-out state that Michael is a compulsive gambler. It is my feeling that he has a problem, regardless of whether it technically fits into the category of quote, addiction, unquote.

Nevertheless, I am reaching out to him. He can ignore what I have to say or he can absorb what I have to say. He might even deny what I have to say, and that would not be out of character given what I have come to know about gambling.

Everyone has heard whispers and innuendo about M.J. and his golf-course gambling. These are not whispers and these are not innuendo.

This is what happened with me...and with us.

Chapter Two

The Coal Miner's Son

Jerry West was always a hero to me. He was from West Virginia. So was I. He was a little ahead of me when it came to his collegiate career at West Virginia University, but I was old enough to catch his professional career with the Los Angeles Lakers.

By the time I was fortunate enough to meet him, he was retired as a player and held his current job as general manager of the Lakers. I was co-owner of the San Diego Sports Arena. One of the perks of running such a facility was that it occasionally enabled me to cross paths with childhood heroes, not to mention numerous modern-day celebrities.

On the day I met Jerry West in our Arena Club, we were sitting with a sportscaster named Lee Hamilton. Coincidentally, all of us were from West Virginia.

It seemed funny. We were like in another world, so far removed from West Virginia in so many ways. One of us, and it should be obvious which one, was a legend. Another was a prominent sports announcer. And there I was an owner of a marquee sports and entertainment venue.

I was sitting there thinking, "Damn, here are three ol' hillbillies who did pretty good for themselves."

Late in the fall of 1991, after Michael Jordan and I had taken our golf betting beyond the realm of reason, I went to see Dr. Lori Stephenson, a clinical psychologist.

I was troubled. I was troubled for myself. I was troubled for Michael Jordan.

I was confused. I was confused about myself. I was confused about Michael Jordan.

My betting had gone beyond where I could lose and pay without doing significant damage to my lifestyle and my family. Jordan's betting had gone beyond where he seemed willing to pay and I didn't understand whether it was because he couldn't or wouldn't.

I didn't really know what I wanted from my therapist. I don't know if I wanted sympathy or advice or understanding or maybe all of everything. I had fought so hard for so long against telling anyone what had been going on in my soul and here and now I was sitting down with a professional. I was determined to bare my soul.

Lori was not an intimidating person at all. She was outgoing and cordial and interested to hear what had brought me to her office. I was nervous as hell, in spite of her assuring way. My mouth was dry and my shirt was wet, almost as if I was standing over some quarter-million dollar putt.

We sat down and we talked, me never guessing this was merely the first of more than 40 one-hour sessions I would spend with her, trying to cope with my burden. At first, I talked. I told her all about myself. And then she talked, and she told me all about myself.

Lori Stephenson told me my entire life was a tapestry of gambles, one risk after another. I didn't get out of the West Virginia hills taking the safest path of least resistance.

This book is a gamble too, one Lori was opposed to me taking and her being a part of. I told her I needed her insight, which has been so important to me as I have struggled to understand myself. I just hope I come off as sensitive to her concerns as she has been to mine.

———

Nothing in my childhood suggested I would ever be in position to get a compliment from Frank Sinatra, play cards with Magic Johnson, present an award to Muhammad Ali or meet Jerry West.

And nothing in my childhood suggested I would ever be in position to engage Michael Jordan, the world's greatest athlete, in games of golf for absolutely outlandish sums of money.

I always had the feeling growing up that I was economically disadvantaged. We had so many kids in the family, eight of us, and so little to go around. We always had food on the table, but the discretionary income was zero. We always had shoes on our feet, but they often had holes in them. What I didn't have drove me harder to succeed, to get through college, to work hard, to get a good job.

All of us kids were born at home in Raysal, West Virginia. Try to find it on a map. I went to show some friends this speck on a map and couldn't find it. It's not too far from Logan down in the southwestern part of the state.

Raysal was and still is more of a coal-mining camp than a town, one of those communities where everything revolves around the mine. I'm talking Deliverance folks who get put away in a hollow—they pronounce it holler—away from legiti- mate towns populated by people who consider themselves above such trash. Everyone in Raysal owes a livelihood to whatever is happening in the mines down below. Sometimes, you have to forge a livelihood in spite of what happens down below.

My father, Daniel Esquinas, was a coal miner. Dad lost the lower part of his left leg in one of those mines down below. He saw a runaway ore cart and he saw a group of guys in its path. He tried to push the miners out of the way, but he got snagged. He gambled and lost. Modern medicine might have saved the leg, but gangrene set in and he had to have a below-the-knee amputation. He was 22 years old, according to my brother Dan, who is sort of the family historian. At least he came away with his life. That was fortuitous for me, because I was not born until he was 42.

It was only natural that my father should work in the coal mines, because that was what my grandfather did as well. He had come to West Virginia through Ellis Island from Spain. It was common in those days for mining interests in the U.S. to recruit Europeans with mining experience. My grandfather came over first and then my grandmother followed in a year or two with the children, including my father.

Coming to America, my family was gambling before I was born.

My father and mother, Betty, met in Logan, the "legitimate" town near Raysal. Mom was an only child whose father, a sheriff named Hy Chafin, was gunned down after chasing a fugitive into what I understood to be a whorehouse. It sounded a little bit like a tale out of the wild west, but it was really just wild West Virginia.

If you thought that sounded like something out of a spaghetti western, wait until I tell you that my family was linked to the real-life Hatfield-McCoy brouhaha. Those weren't fictional battles. They were reality in those days in our neck of the woods. One of my grandmothers was related to the Hatfields.

Our house in Raysal was ultra-modest rather than ultra-modern. We had three bedrooms, one for the boys, one for the girls and one for Mom and Dad. It was a small, simple house, with a coal stove in the living room for heat. We had a small kitchen, a small living room and a little dining area. It may seem surprising, but we did have indoor toilets. All those years in tight quarters made us a close-knit family. We're probably tighter today than ever.

Dad was always working on the house, trying to make it better. I almost died at an early age because I fell on a nail while Dad was on one of his do-it-yourself projects. It took almost 45 minutes to get to a hospital and I almost bled to death. I was too young to remember much about it, but the whole experience had to leave a lasting impression in my subconscious.

One thing about the family was that living quarters might have been a whole lot tighter, except the eight kids were spread out a little bit. My brother Rob and I were twins, the sixth and seventh kids. There was a seven-year gap between the fifth child and us.

My therapist felt that being a twin and being towards the end of eight children affected me strongly. She felt that it gave me a sense of not being cared for and having to go outside my family to meet my needs for emotion and stimulation.

I guess this need for stimulation, and maybe self-approval, are part of what causes us gambling types to take the risks we do.

Mother wanted something better for her children, so the family moved to Columbus, Ohio, when I was five. The potential advantages were worth the risk for her, but Dad never was comfortable after he got out of the mines. He started selling insurance, but he was out of his element. He never adjusted to what he considered to be the fast track of city life in Columbus.

My parents divorced after 26 years of marriage when I was 10, another traumatic twist for an impressionable youth. I cannot help but think that Dad's discomfort with the move to Columbus had a lot to do with it, that and the pressures associated with the struggle to survive economically with eight children. The strain got to be too much on the relationship.

Regardless of what he was doing, my father worked hard and smart. There were lengthy periods of time in West Virginia when he never saw the sun, because he would go down into the mine before it was up and come out after it had set. He would come home and fall asleep with his clothes on. He would be too exhausted to even toss and turn.

There were times when I was working in the bowels of the San Diego Sports Arena when I could relate, in a way, to Dad. I'd get there before the sun was up and leave after the sun went down. And I would be too tired to toss and turn. Realistically, though, it's a little far-fetched to parallel a sports arena with a coal mine.

Dad wasn't into things like golf, which he considered a little frivolous. However, his artificial leg did not keep him from an enjoyment of dancing and he was a little bit of a drinker. He dressed well, and I took that from him. He never had a big wardrobe, but he was meticulous about his presentation, very conscious of his looks.

After the divorce, he took a little gamble of his own and moved to California. Mom, by then, worked for the Ohio Department of Transportation as an administrator in the real estate division. She was with the department for 30 years. She worked hard too. She was driven to provide both emotional and financial stability and to instill pride in the family unit.

I shouldn't slight my mother and say I got my work ethic from my father. That would not be fair. However, it would be safe to say I got my drive to make something better of life from my mother, regardless of the risk.

———

Six of my siblings are still in Columbus, which remains the family hub. I have one sister, Mary Jo, who lives in Oregon. My parents are both deceased, but the family stays close to that homestead in Ohio.

After my mother's death, one of my dreams was to establish a new central gathering place for the family. I wanted a log cabin. Actually, what I built was more a log home than a log cabin.

With everyone back in Ohio, it did not make much sense to build it in Southern California. That wasn't the atmosphere I wanted anyway. I wanted a setting with trees and hills and wildlife and maybe a pond. I wanted the closest thing to West Virginia without being in West Virginia.

I found just such a place in an area called Hocking Hills, about an hour south of Columbus at the tip of Appalachia. It's almost 30 acres and sits up on a hill overlooking a pond.

This was a place which would take me and my family back to both our West Virginia and Ohio roots. The cabin has become our core place to gather, nurture family relations and revisit family history.

I did the funding and my brother Rob and brother-in-law Nick DiPasquale worked as on-site construction coordinators. What we came up with was a 3,000-square-foot "cabin" with a master bedroom, spare bedroom, over-sized bunkroom, loft, large deck and a great room for gathering everyone together.

The great room has a great couch. I call it my "Jordan Couch." It's a nice high-end couch, soft with baseball stitching. It has deep, rich chocolate-brown leather, almost the color of M.J.'s skin. It's symbolic to me of Jordan's very refined taste. Of course, I used money I won from him to buy it. It will always be part of the cabin's folklore.

My wife Kerry's signature contribution didn't have the sizzle of a trophy couch won from gambling earnings. She went the romantic route. She wanted and got a heart-shaped bathtub.

The project was started in 1988 and completed in time for Christmas in 1990. We have all been together since then for Christmas, Thanksgiving and Fourth of July. Counting nieces and nephews, immediate family totals 41 when we are all together for a holiday. All my siblings have their own keys so they can use the place whether I'm back there or not.

My wife Kerry and I and daughter Felicity go to the cabin whenever we vacation. We don't go to Acapulco or those other glitzy places. The last thing I need when I'm on a vacation from the Sports Arena is to travel. I want my senses to go inward. This is the place for me to retreat when I want to go back to my roots and my values, where salaries, titles, name-dropping and other status symbols are not a part of day-to-day living.

In a sense, the cabin is kind of a memorial for my mother and a museum for the family. I'm the custodian of our family photos, so I have enlarged the nicest ones and put them up around the cabin. One of my favorites is of Hy Chafin, my mother's father, the lawman who never should have chased that fugitive into the whorehouse. Another is a picture of my mother and father posing starry-eyed with their first child. We treasure our family history.

■■■■

I was in seventh grade when I discovered money could be made from golf. This discovery came in a very modest and very basic form. It had nothing to do with watching Jack Nicklaus, our biggest local legend except maybe Woody Hayes, sink some big-money putt.

It seemed all of the Catholic boys in north Columbus were caddies at the Winding Hollow Country Club, incongruously, perhaps, a Jewish club. I joined their ranks, usually hitching a ride the eight miles from the Linden area to the golf course.

To help put food on the table and clothes on my back, I had started working at a young age. I did all the things young kids can do to make some bucks. I mowed grass and weeded gardens and washed dishes and delivered newspapers. This was all fine with me, because the whole family had to contribute to the group welfare.

When I started caddying, I went all out. There were back-to-back years when I caddied for more rounds of golf than anyone else. I'd go 54 holes some days, beginning at 6 a.m. and lugging clubs until dark. I'd take bags no one else would carry, like maybe for members who might be pains in the you know where.

I'd carry four bags at a time on mega-hack ladies day, walking down the middle of the fairway and letting them come to me for clubs. I don't know if I have broad shoulders from carrying so much weight or if I could carry so much weight because I have broad shoulders. Regardless, I did it because I needed all the money I could earn.

When I first moved into Columbus, my neighborhood was all white. In the next four or five years, coinciding with the civil rights movement, it became a black neighborhood.

"There you go," Lori said, "You are already one of the last born in a hectic and now divided household and the neighborhood becomes predominantly black. You don't fit because you're white."

I never quite looked at it like that, but it made sense. I was white, poor and feeling either displaced or misplaced.

My experience growing up with blacks has actually been good for me. I developed a rapport with them, an understanding, which has helped me both personally and professionally. I have always had very cordial relationships with black artists and athletes at the Sports Arena. And, of course, I was able to assimilate very quickly with Michael Jordan and his buddies. It all goes back to growing up in the Linden area.

It made no difference who lived in the Linden area, it was bad. Railroad tracks separated it from the better part of town. It was literally on the wrong side of the tracks.

The Linden area is notoriously bad now, deeply entrenched in poverty, but it's still my neighborhood. Even today when I am in Columbus, I go back to the old neighborhood. One of my financial goals was to make $100,000 a year by the time I was 30 and I did that, but I have always tried to keep my success in perspective. I've never forgotten where I came from. I walk around the neighborhood and I feel the edge of economic discomfort. I find my visits to be both healthy and motivating.

Most of the guys I ran with have moved out of the Linden area, guys like Mike and John Susi, Jim Hart, Pat Hatem, David

Kimberly, Tim Moone and Chris and Terry Arnold, but my best buddy, Michael Yurkovic, still lives only a couple of blocks from the neighborhood. I have tremendous regard for Michael, a city employee who is happily married with two bright boys. He alone is a good reason to return for visits because in many ways we are as close as I am with my own brothers and, simply stated, he may be the most decent human being I've ever met.

My first cash-on-the-line gambling experience was with a kid named Henry from one of the first black families who moved into the neighborhood. I had always enjoyed card games at home, and I got so I could kick my brother Dan's butt and he was nine years older than I. But that wasn't gambling. Henry produced dice one day and taught me how to shoot on the sidewalk in front of his house. Gambling is frequently introduced at an early age, today more so than yesterday, and this was my first encounter.

I must have been in the sixth grade, maybe the fifth. Mom had taken out a loan on a bicycle so I could take over a morning newspaper route I had inherited from Mike and Victor Yurkovic. The bike probably cost $42, which was an awful lot to us, especially in those days.

Between the newspaper route and mowing some lawns, I always had a little bit of coin in my pocket. I caught onto craps and beat this kid out of like $4. He wanted to rev up the betting, got frantic and ran out of money. I got him out of his comfort zone and he was pissed.

In retrospect, I recognized a lot of these traits when I finally sat down with my therapist after M.J. and I got out of control. Henry was chasing his losses, as M.J. and I would both do. The "feeding frenzy" feeling is hard to shake. And I had made what to me at the time was a big score which whetted my appetite for more of the same.

I was happy about my good fortune. I went home and bragged to my older brothers and sisters. The kid was so unhappy with me that he came later that night and stole my bike.

Somebody saw him riding it and my older brother Dan confronted his father, but Henry denied it. He had hidden the bike, but Dan got a lucky tip and found the hiding place.

A week later, I had both the money and my bike. I was lucky. I ended up on the right side of a gambling experience, as I would later with M.J.

That was my first taste of gambling, but I really learned about it in the caddy shack when I was in the seventh or eighth grade. There was always a card game of some sort, usually with a whopping 25-cent ante. What's more, there was a basketball court where wagers could be made. We found ways to fill the inevitable dead time when there were no bags to carry. I learned how to curse too and I learned a little bit about women, or at least girls, from the hierarchy, the older boys. Put 30 to 40 hormone-spouting Catholic boys in a confined area and I guarantee talk will get around to girls.

From the viewpoint of a caddy, I also learned about golf and golf gambling. There were some awful good golfers in that club and both the pro and the assistant pros would use me as a caddy when they went to play in pro-ams. There was always gambling of some sort going on. I never knew exactly what the stakes were, but I learned how matches were put together.

I also realized that golf from a caddy's viewpoint was no way to go.

"You were exposed to wealth and how comfortable that is," Lori would say. "You were thinking, 'I don't want to be the caddy. I want to be the one who has the caddy.' By the way, you didn't fit there either. You were Catholic."

———

One of the older boys in the caddy shack was a guy named Bo. He was sort of the kingpin. He had an uncanny memory for sports statistics, told great stories and mastered the use of the

F-word. He was good at everything we all liked to do, especially the gambling.

Bo took this gambling thing in a different direction. He started booking bets.

Later, when I was at Ohio State University, I used to make bets on college basketball with Bo. I was really into college hoops. I knew all the starting lineups, and who was injured, on the Top 20 teams. I'd bet $50 or $100 a game, but I'd have money on eight, nine, 10 games. I'd have swings of $250 to $1,000. My appetite for gambling was already stretching my wallet. I didn't see it at the time, but I was already betting far more than was sensible when my expenses were weighed against my income. Relatively speaking, I was out of control even back then, without the stimulus of a Jordan to rev me up.

I always worked hard and had cash, but never a whole lot. I hit a home run on one series of bets and paid a quarter's room and board at the frat house. Big hits, Lori told me later, were part of the hook that dragged people into compulsive gambling. You know, like the $4 killing I made playing craps against the black kid. Now I was quite pleased with myself that I had won enough money to wipe out a quarter's room and board.

A little bit of success creates an aura of invulnerability and I was winning more than I lost, in both gambling and life.

Bad days follow good, however, and I dropped $1,200 I didn't have. I had to pay Bo, so I went to a bank and borrowed the money. I disguised it as a student loan. Borrowing money to fuel the addiction was another negative sign I didn't recognize until my therapist later hit me over the head with it.

I kept right on betting. And Bo got into trouble with me. I beat him for $1,500 and he said he couldn't pay me. Here was a bookie saying he couldn't pay me. He said he'd been busted and lost his cash and I knew that wasn't true. I'd gone through the exercise with the bank to pay my debt to him and now he was avoiding me. I was pissed. Really pissed.

I went over with Rob, my 6-foot-5, 260-pound twin brother

who had been an All-American high school football player. We knocked on the door of Bo's apartment. We could hear him coming to the door, probably to look through the peep hole and stare into the glaring eyes of my very formidable and very pissed brother. Nothing happened.

I gave the nod to Rob and he started kicking the door down. It was reminding me of when we were growing up and I would sic him on neighborhood bullies who were fucking with me. Bo opened the door very quickly. I walked in, Rob already having Bo sitting on the couch, all three of us were pissed. I handed him my payment coupon book from the bank.

"You owe me the money," I said, "so you can take this and make the payments."

I noticed his golf clubs propped in a corner.

"The first payment you miss," I said, "I'm gonna come and get your clubs and Rob here is going to have a field day on your head."

Bo made the payments. I had no hard feelings. It was just business. That was the only time I've ever felt a little like a mobster.

———

I had a burning desire to succeed. I needed a college education. I had not been a model student through high school, partially because I did not have any academic role models in my family, but I realized I had to get beyond high school to get beyond my roots. I saw it as my only way out.

In high school, I was a smart kid but an under-achiever. I had started high school at St. Francis DeSales, a Catholic school after eight years in St. Augustine grade school. Private schools are expensive, but they cut deals with the economically disad-vantaged to decrease tuition. My mother said she would cover the tuition, but we had to buy our own pants, shirts and ties. Maybe that was where I got onto the tie gig. I have about 400 of them now, all silk and all by chic designers. Most of them would have been laughed at by my high school buddies.

I only lasted at St. Francis through my sophomore year. I was a little radical, a troublemaker, a comedian with a smart mouth. They could deal with dumb kids more easily than they could with a smart aleck with good grades.

When I got called onto the carpet, the head disciplinarian, Mr. Flannery, sternly said: "If you don't straighten up, we're not going to invite you back."

He had gotten his hackles up because I had not shown up for detention he had imposed. And I had gotten my hackles up because someone else had done whatever the dirty deed had been. I wasn't going to pay the dues for it.

"Don't worry," I said. "I'm not coming back."

"Once again," Lori said. "You didn't fit."

I switched to Brookhaven High School, a public school directly across the street. I was happy. I had kept all my buddies from St. Francis, all the kids I had grown up with and all the kids I had caddied with. I was invited to return to the Catholic school for my senior year, but I said no thank you.

That was both stubborn and brash, but that was the way I was. Maybe the way I am.

Interestingly, I was invited to work on the committee for the 20th reunion of St. Francis's Class of '73. That would have been my graduating class at St. Francis if I hadn't been graduated from Brookhaven instead. I had always felt a part of that class and I was flattered that the feeling was mutual. I accepted.

Take that, shrink. I fit. For a change.

———

When it came to dancing to the tune of a different drummer, I was Nureyev. When I was still in high school, I got into transcendental meditation. How many high school kids get into TM? Not many.

I studied Maharishi Mahesh Yogi, probably the best-known yogi in the western world, whose book, "The Bhagavad Gita," has been a companion through the years. A high school friend got me interested. I started TM in 1973 and Hatha Yoga postures in 1974.

"There you were doing something different again," Lori said. "High school boys in Ohio didn't do that. You were on the outside so much that you went inside yourself. You wanted control, internal control."

Shit, I was just trying to find myself. I haven't missed a day since then. I do it every morning and every evening, without fail. That says something about control and discipline, but I guess it also says something about compulsive behavior, though I would say this is a positive form of compulsion. Lori agreed with me.

Whereas I had been hyper, I found that this settled me down on both a physiological and psychological level. It kept me focused. It kept outside influences such as drugs and alcohol away. The only vice it fell short on was gambling.

When I was older and working a lot of hours, it helped a lot with stress. It helped keep me young in terms of my thinking. And it brought calm to my surroundings and helped me make tough decisions with peace of mind.

It helps keep me right-on with my thinking about golf too. I'm not a guy to go out there and drink beer and hit the ball around. I have a certain emotional, philosophical experience every time I go out there. It might seem flaky or weird, but there's more to it than just knocking the ball around the course. The fact that I am deeply entrenched in the game gives me an advantage.

I've always contended that I psychologically beat Jordan. I could paint him into the corner with my mental game. Golf is not like basketball, where you can win by playing harder and exerting more energy. You cannot force the ball in golf. I was able to manage my stress and decrease it. I was able to do things with my psyche that I couldn't do with my body.

TM helped me and I think it can help any individual needing stress management, but I've never been evangelical about it. I didn't push it with my buddies, not in high school, not in college and not now, because I know they'd think it was freaky-deaky.

———

There was never a trace of doubt that I was going to go to college. It wasn't forced upon me. My mother never forced the issue and my father thought most education with the liberal course titles and the loose lifestyle was a waste of time. In spite of the lack of parental pressure, my desire for an education was deeply internalized by my home situation. I knew I had to go to college to get where I wanted life to take me, though I was not sure yet where that might be.

Coming out of high school, I ended up at West Hills Community College in Coalinga, California, which got hit by that big earthquake in 1988. This rather bold and brash cross-country move was also a risk, as my therapist would point out.

If this seems strange, it was. My twin brother, Rob, didn't have the grades to get any scholarship offers for his football, so we went to the only college that would have us both. The football coach just happened to be the golf coach.

In truth, I would like to have been in Rob's version of cleats. I would like to have been the football star. I envisioned the Friday night heroics Rob enjoyed, but I was on the outside looking in. A physical examination in the seventh grade revealed that I had a heart murmur. Although I competed in grade school, that was it for a high school athletic career in physically demanding sports such as football and basketball. I had always been an athlete, usually the first guy picked on the playgrounds, and now I was a spectator.

"This was a key thing for you," Lori said. "You'd always been an athlete, but now you weren't allowed to compete. You were smart, but let's face it, you don't get kudos as a male in Ohio for being smart. I don't think you were consciously mad or jealous of your brother, but I think this increased your drive to achieve something of your own. There's an element here as to why gambling on sports becomes important to you. You don't get to prove yourself earlier in life, so what better way as an adult than a golf course? You fast forward and now you're competing on the golf course with a guy who may be the athlete of the century."

Rob and I were always competing, always in physical combat, and his glories were mine. I enjoyed seeing him succeed, but I was disappointed he ignored his academics and didn't give himself a better chance. A knee injury inhibited his collegiate career and he never played at a four-year university. John Johnson, who would later become Buster Douglas's manager, got him a tryout with the Cincinnati Bengals, but he didn't make the cut.

Both Esquinas brothers were finished with physically-combatative sports ahead of their time, but I still had golf. Rob has taken up the game now and become a golf junkie himself, but he did not touch a club when he was younger.

Between West Hills and my return to Ohio State University, I took a detour through Fairfield, Iowa, and spent eight months at the Maharishi International University in the winter of 1974-75. It had previously been Parsons College. I helped with the physical labor involved in getting the place established. I was able to spend limited time with the Maharishi, who visited campus, and reinforce my feelings about TM.

When I got to Ohio State, I still had both golf and education on my mind. I may have been the No. 1 guy on the West Hills golf team, but I couldn't seem to see the bottom rung on the ladder when I got back to Columbus. I started playing around at Scarlet, the OSU golf course, thinking I was hot stuff. The guys at Ohio State were good. John Cook was on that team and he's one of the best players on the PGA Tour today.

Ironically, M.J. and I ran into John one day when we were playing at Bear Creek, a Jack Nicklaus course in one of Southern California's inland valleys. John didn't remember me because I had done something smart and quit the OSU team before I had actually started.

From those days in the caddy shack, I had wanted to be a professional golfer. I decided I better bet on a sure thing for a change. I bet on the certainty of what an education might provide as opposed to the uncertainty of pro golf.

One of my high school friends who dated back to my caddying days, Pat Croswell, never got a degree, but he is now the pro at Oakland Hills in Michigan, one of the country's premier golf clubs. I admit there are times when I am jealous of Pat.

Typical of me, when I realized I was not going to be on the golf team at OSU, I quit the sport as well. I wanted to focus on my education and get my B.S. in education. Golf was a serious distraction.

"That's typical of you," Lori said. "All or nothing. Once you decided college was your way out, you blocked everything else out. You didn't even have any love relationships during that time, you were so single-minded."

Love relationships? I didn't have time for love, but I spent time with plenty of women who could tolerate my machismo, womanizing ways.

Stuff like that was part of college, right? If I was going to be in college, I was going to be a collegian. I wanted the classic college experience. I didn't want to commute to classes from home. I decided to join the Lambda Chi Alpha fraternity and lived on frat row for three years. I didn't have any money, but I had guts. Money usually gets you a lot further in fraternity life than guts. I still ended up on the frat council and vice-president of my house.

Lori sighed.

"Without any money," she said, "you had no business

joining a fraternity. You were just determined you were going to fit."

Even though I wasn't staying at home, I was still home in Columbus. Most of my boyhood buddies were still around. Not too many had gone on to college. I wasn't about to abandon friendships because I was a frat guy and they were a rat pack.

It was funny, really. All my old friends, like my brother Rob and Nibby, Yurky and John Susi, Yinger, Cua, Trout, Delco, Disabato would come down to the frat house wearing blue jeans with holes in them and scruffy T-shirts. With them, it was fuck this and fuck that. They were the blue collar guys mixing it up with the blue bloods.

My frat brothers called them The Dead End Kids. When they were around, it was kind of like Spanky and Our Gang visit Ozzie and Harriet. These guys didn't think they had had any fun if they had not picked a fight with the fraternity next door or any other nose-in-the-air preppy who ventured too near. I don't even want to talk about The Dead End Kids and the sorority down the street, because hassling pretty co-eds was their ultimate high. Rob was crazy then. He'd come in and say, "What'll it be tonight? Fighting or fucking?"

The Dead End Kids actually elevated our status in the Greek community to a more macho level. My frat brothers adopted them and we used them as occasional ringers in athletic events. I was pretty proud of the guys from the old neighborhood, managing to fit where none of us fit.

As bad as we thought we were, the guys who followed us must have been worse. The university closed the house down a year after I was graduated in 1978. It has since been reinstated and I have worked extensively in fund-raising, which I spent all of my college years doing on my own behalf.

Some of my best friends today came from the frat where I didn't fit...Kirstein, Perks, and Hunt to name a few.

I worked all the way through OSU, begging, stealing and borrowing money to make ends meet. I worked for the Columbus

Parks and Recreation Department, sometimes part-time and sometimes full-time. I worked for an inner-city rec center. I worked wherever I could work. I still came out of school $5,000 in debt, but that was a lot better than some others have done. And I've paid back my loans. Writing that last check in 1982 felt very good.

When I was graduated from Ohio State, I interviewed with Proctor and Gamble in Cincinnati. That would have been a nice, safe place to work, right down the road from my home town. My mother thought it was wonderful. Her first and only child who made it through college would be working for a big company near home.

That wasn't me. That made too much sense. My choice was to go to a small company in a big town rather than a big company in a smaller town. I first went to New Jersey before stopping in to New York City, the biggest of towns. I wanted the fast pace and the sizzle of New York. I took a job with a small direct marketing agency.

Another gamble. Another win. If I had not done that, I never would have met Harry Cooper.

Chapter Three

The Beginning

When Harry Cooper and I bought the San Diego Sports
Arena, only one thing was on our minds. We did not want to
merely get into the arena business. Far from it. Our game plan
was to get into the state-of-the-art arena business. We wanted to
be the guys who brought National Basketball Association and
National Hockey League franchises to San Diego.

We knew we could not get this done with the existing Sports
Arena, at least not if that venue was to be any more than a
temporary home while a new arena was being built. Anyone
who has been in the old arena knows it is not exactly state-of-
the-art. We could pump money into it and make it better, but we
could not make it good enough for either the NBA or NHL as a
permanent home for franchises.

Just a few days after we completed the acquisition of the
Sports Arena on June 16, 1989, we were confronted by a
decision. We had to put up $100,000 to be sanctioned by the
NBA for a summer all-star game. This was to be a charity affair
to benefit Multiple Sclerosis.

Key managers of the Sports Arena at the time were not in
favor of it. It had not been successful the previous year, so they
thought it was too risky.

Harry and I kicked it around. We didn't really have a choice.

Here we had just been announced as the new owners of the arena. We had stood in front of a media mob and declared our intention to not only use the current arena as a springboard to a new arena but to go to the mat for NBA and NHL franchises.

We even had a motto: "San Diego back in the NBA."

I know, that was not the catchiest of jingles. We weren't thinking either fast or fancy. We just wanted our most basic of intentions known.

How could we defend our efforts to attract the NBA if we wouldn't front $100,000 to bring in an all-star game? It was much too early to back away from that kind of risk.

We scheduled it for August, two days after Magic Johnson sponsored a similar game in Los Angeles. We hoped we could get a few of the big-name guys to hang around and come down the road for our game. I contacted Lon Rosen, Magic's agent, and he told me Magic was all but 100 per cent set to play. Rosen had to give himself squirming room because these guys were all but 100 per cent reliable when it came to freebie commitments such as this.

With Magic as committed as he could be, I could think of only one other superstar we needed to assure success.

Guess who? Michael Jordan was the other half of the biggest duo in sports, when it came to box office.

I needed help. Keith Padgett, the executive director of the local MS chapter and event promoter, was in touch with Michael through his schedule coordinator. Michael too was all but 100 per cent set. It would turn out I wouldn't need help getting Michael in the future.

I was excited. I felt Harry and I had stepped right in and made an impact. I felt we had gained instant credibility. We had a long way to go to get the building into shape, but we had put together our first marquee event and the ink was barely dry on the contracts.

I knew this was nothing like the mid-season all-star game, with all that hype and hoopla. It was a mere exhibition, but very few of them are officially sanctioned. The players run to them in posses and play cards and golf and have fun and throw in a pickup basketball game.

Fans don't care. They want to see the big names, particularly in unfortunate cities which don't have teams of their own. Undeservedly, San Diego was among those cities.

I didn't care that it wasn't a real game either. I loved basketball in any form. And maybe this game would be a vehicle that would get us rolling toward real basketball in San Diego.

The game went off great. Both Magic and Michael were 100 per cent there, Michael scoring 43 points. Not a soul in the world remembers who won, or even who was on which team. We had "drafted" the players into two teams with no particular geographic alignment. The sellout crowd of 13,105 wanted virtuoso performances from the stars and it got what it wanted. Our credibility had gone up a few notches in the community.

I ran into Smokey Gaines at the post-game party at a Mission Valley hotel. Smokey had been basketball coach at the University of Detroit and San Diego State University and he has the garrulous way of knowing darn near anyone who ever bounced a ball in his lifetime.

"Hey man," Gaines said, grabbing me by the arm, "let me introduce you to Michael."

Michael? Michael Jackson being off somewhere playing with his toys, I did not need to ask which Michael. When it comes to basketball, there is only one. And Michael Jordan was in a roped off section of the room with half of San Diego hanging onto him like Christmas ornaments. I was very new in the arena business, but I already had grown sensitive to giving celebrities some room. I did not want to become just one more person imposing on Jordan's space.

"I told Michael about you," Gaines said. "I told him you

were a good golfer. I told him you liked to play. He asked me to introduce you to him."

I was wary. I couldn't be sure my friend Smokey wasn't blowing some smoke. He had a little bit of bluster to him. He came to San Diego a few years earlier to coach basketball at State and said he would move to Japan and open a big man's store if he didn't get the team to the Final Four. He never reached the Final Four and he never moved to Japan either. Now he owned a night spot in town.

Once again, he tugged on my arm.

"Come on," he said. "Let's go meet him."

This was sounding interesting. It was almost Walter Mittyesque. I couldn't play basketball with Michael Jordan any more than I could play football with Joe Montana or baseball with Tony Gwynn, but I knew I could play golf with him.

We walked into the roped off area and Smokey sauntered up to Jordan as casually as he would walk into his own saloon.

"This is Richard E," Gaines said, "the guy I told you about earlier. The guy that owns the arena? He's a good golfer... like you."

Jordan shook my hand. He had a whimsical look on his face, sort of like a cat eyeing a canary who didn't realize why he had been invited to lunch. Actually, he was probably looking at me more as a pigeon than a canary.

"Nice game," I said. "I really appreciate your coming down here for us."

Jordan laughed. It had been a nice game, as playground basketball goes, but the accolade was something he probably heard after every game in every city. I do think he knew the thank you was sincere. I've always wanted to make artists feel appreciated when they came to my house.

Nevertheless, this was how our relationship started. It began as all relationships begin, with small talk and gab. He seemed sincere and personable. We probably even commented on what a nice day it had been. Maybe talk about the weather got us into how perfect the weather was for golf, as if we needed such stimulus. We had each caught the scent of a fellow gambler.

"What kind of clubs you got?" I asked.

"Where do you play?" he wondered.

That's how the golf started too, with small talk and gab. It did not take long to get feisty. I knew right away that Michael was competitive. And I knew right away he was not the type to play for who bought the hot dogs at the 19th hole.

"Michael," I said, "I have a six handicap. I hear that's right about where you're at. I've got a tee time tomorrow. If you want to show up and play, I'll give you the best game you can get in Southern California. I'll play for whatever you want to play for."

My Latin machismo was coming out and I could tell I had gotten his attention. Gamblers have a way of honing in on each other. I knew he was a player and he knew I was a player. It's an instinctive thing.

"Man," he said, "my clubs are up north in Laguna Niguel. That's two hours away."

"Michael," I said, "I'm just telling you we have a time if you want a game. Maybe you can find someone to get your clubs for you."

"I'll see," he said.

"Do what you can do," I said. "If you can make it, it would be great. If you can't make it, maybe we can do it some other time. Anyway, thank you again for being here tonight."

I wasn't thinking in terms of getting down major bets and starting a mano-a-mano which would take us from coast to coast to crazy. I wasn't even *really* a hard-core fan. I just wanted to play golf with the man.

Who wouldn't?

━━━

My telephone was ringing early in the morning. Smokey Gaines was on the line.

"Richard E," he said, "Jordan's gonna be there."

"Fine, Smoke," I said. "We'll be there."

I had an 8 a.m. tee time at Stardust Country Club with my regular group. Stardust is a 27-hole resort course which sprawls behind a hotel in Mission Valley in the heart of San Diego. It gets a mix of members and hotel guests, and the regulars it gets are some of the hottest golfers in San Diego...or the U.S., for that matter.

Phil Mickelson, the new phenom on the PGA Tour, honed his game there. Scott Simpson, the former U.S. Open champion, plays there and so does Scott's father, a damned good player himself. Lon Hinkle, who's had some success on the tour, plays there. And there are a lot of young bucks around, all of them hoping maybe they'll get a break.

Stardust has a whole posse of notoriously good golfers who are notoriously good gamblers. Evel Kneivel plays there and he's been about as big a gambler as there is around, some of the stunts he's pulled. There's always action around.

They have one bunch I respectfully call the Banditos, guys like Howard Matheny, Steve Turner, Eddie Cuff, Mike Horton and a cast of thousands. Matheny, a former San Diego amateur champion, is the ringleader. It's gone down a bit the last couple of years, but they used to go off at 11 a.m. with three, four, five groups, all kinds of bets from one group to another. It wasn't real big stuff, but you never really knew.

These guys called my regular group "Closed Shop," because we'd often go off on our own. I liked the Banditos and they liked me, probably because I was easy on the first tee, as they say in gambling circles. I liked the challenge of a fair game as opposed to seeking a betting advantage.

My usual foursome included Fred Sarno, Ron Heitzinger and Eric Weinberg, all of us in the same age range with similar golf games. We got so close we would take our games on the road, a moving feast of golf, and play in Tahoe and San Francisco and Phoenix and even Acapulco.

"It's rare and unique," Fred said to me once, "that four guys can be so even that we don't even need to handicap to neutralize our games."

That was the way we were, all completely different in size and temperament but all relatively even on the bottom line...the scorecard. We all had a few bucks to gamble on the course, but we'd keep the bets to like five ways for $10 each or five ways for $20 each. We'd rev it up a bit when we took our act on the road.

A typical five-way bet for our group would be a unit on the front, meaning whatever we decided to bet, and maybe two units each on the back nine and the overall 18. That would be five different units...or five different ways. A golfer who got behind could press, or start a new bet, for another unit at any point in the match. We always made presses automatic when one golfer got two holes behind.

Heitzinger is our numbers guy. Not only did he always know where he stood in a given match, I think he knows where he stands against everyone he has played against from the first time he teed up a golf ball.

Ron's a big guy, 44 years old now, who's a substance abuse expert with special expertise in the field of college and professional athletics. His company, Heitzinger and Associates, is headquartered in Madison, Wisconsin, but Ron lives in San Diego now. In fact, he can see Stardust from where he lives.

I have a lot in common with this guy. We both got interested in golf as caddies, we're both from Big Ten universities (he's from Wisconsin), we're both twins and we're both crazy when it comes to golf. He kept track from Jan. 1, 1988 to Jan. 1, 1992 and he played 525 rounds of golf.

Sarno was originally a Las Vegas guy. His father, who's deceased now, built and owned Caesar's Palace and Circus Circus, two of the biggest places on The Strip. He knows the gaming industry and gambling protocol as well as anybody. Freddy lives in La Jolla now and manufactures a line of golf attire.

You know what happened the first time Michael Jordan wore one of Freddy's shirts? He spilled mustard on it. Nike would like that. Maybe he did it on purpose.

Eric, a New York guy, came to the game a little later than the rest of us. He got strokes for awhile, but not once he got it in gear. He's not as long off the tee as the rest of us, except maybe Freddy, but he's a killer around the green with his chipping and putting.

Did Eric catch up?

One year, we kept track of birdies, eagles, fairways hit, greens in regulation and scoring average. We put it into a software program and Eric spit out a report every week. It gave us another level of interest and competition. We'd have arguments over whether a ball at the edge of the green was on or off. It was a big deal to us. Plus, we had $3,000 in a pot.

"We'd compare our stats to the PGA Tour," Eric said. "The only place we weren't competitive was in scoring."

And Weinberg, that Eric-come-lately, was our scoring leader with like a 77-and-change average. Freddy had the highest percentage of fairways hit and I led in birdies, eagles and greens in regulation.

This was the group gathering at Stardust, unaware that a new chapter in our lives was about to begin. I told them that Michael Jordan might be joining us and they looked at me like they were going to believe it when they saw it. I could sense their excitement and I could understand their skepticism. I was both excited and skeptical myself.

"Smokey called this morning and said Jordan would be here," I said. "That's all I know. I talked to him for awhile last night after the game and told him we had a starting time. I don't know if he's showing, but Smokey says he is."

If Jordan was showing, one of us—and it obviously wasn't going to be me—was sitting. The guys tossed coins. Heitzinger lost. That was our first "gamble" involving Jordan and he wasn't even there yet.

I was on the driving range warming up when I heard the buzz running through the clubhouse. I would get used to this. There was always a frenzy in the clubhouse and around the first tee when M.J. showed up. And the man was there.

Heitzinger laughed about this phenomenon.

"We'd go to the first tee and I'd watch what was happening with the crowd," he said. "I wouldn't even watch the tee shots. Here I'd be on the first tee with Michael Jordan and there'd be a mob of jealous people wondering who in heck those guys with Jordan were."

Jordan came up and we started with niceties, like wasn't it nice to be on a golf course when the rest of the world was working. We got to the point when we got to the first tee, the ritualistic site where the game and the bet is negotiated. My chemistry started to churn and I felt a sense of euphoria. I was always like that to a certain degree, but now I was negotiating with the world's greatest athlete.

Later I would learn that this rush was part of the addiction, part of the craving which needed fulfilling. It didn't matter whether one was on the first tee or at a betting window at a race track. Hell, I thought I was just nervous.

I opened our first negotiation.

"What do you want to play for?" I asked.

For all I knew, he easily could have said five ways for $10,000 each.

"Whatever you want," he said. "Name it."

This was the Jordan psyche at work. This was trash talk on the greensward instead of on the basketball court. I would learn later that bravado and machismo are very much part of a gambler's makeup. This was my first taste of M.J.'s gamesmanship and I came back with a little bravado and machismo of my own.

"OK, Michael," I said, "you haven't played with me and I haven't played with you. No one's hustling or being hustled. We'll play $500 five ways with two-down automatic presses."

I smiled.

"And we'll play even," I said.

In your face, I thought to myself. I knew I'd put some lead in his pencil.

I was bending over to tee up my ball when he came back at me.

"I hope the pressure of playing with me doesn't bother you," he said.

I'm sure he was thinking, "Touche. I've got this guy."

All the while, this buddy of Jordan's, Adolph Shiver, was yakking and blabbing. We would get used to Adolph, reluctantly so.

Off we went. The golf course was not a social setting to Jordan. It was not a place to drink beer or marvel at fairway-side homes or exchange pleasantries about family and friends. Heitzinger remembered that he told Jordan about his job that first day but he didn't remember that Jordan had bothered to ask. M.J. wanted to focus on golf.

You know that stupid joke about the guy named George who has a heart attack and dies on a golf course? From then on, it was hit the ball and drag George? If George had died in our group, M.J. would have been asking if maybe we couldn't drag him a little faster.

Later, after I had played many, many rounds with Michael, I realized he liked to control the tempo of the game. In a sense, it was a little like basketball. M.J. wanted to move and move quickly. He consciously and subconsciously wanted rhythm to the round.

A light bulb went on in my head. If I could set the tempo of the round, I could take him out of his game. Tactics like that work in basketball, right? How many times have disciplined teams upset teams with superior talent by controlling the pace? Controlling the tempo and pace would give me a distinct advantage.

How would I accomplish this? I would drive the golf cart!

That would literally put me in the driver's seat.

There are other ways too. You can take a bit longer to set up to hit and agonize a little longer trying to read putts. You can slow things down on the tee by fidgeting with the scorecard.

I had tried controlling the tempo in a different direction with Freddy Sarno, who is bar none the slowest player on the face of the earth. I wanted to speed things up with him. You know, hurrying to your ball and hitting quickly. The grass could grow a couple of inches in the time it would take Freddy to play a par-five. Freddy's so slow we would be three holes behind the group ahead of us. I would get out ahead of the group and act impatient and try to speed him up and take him out of his tempo. He caught on very quickly and hated it when he wasn't the one behind the wheel of his cart.

Jordan's comfortable tempo was exactly the opposite of Freddy's. When he was driving the cart, he would get into a quick groove. He would hit and be at his ball and ready to hit again. He controlled the game and you'd better keep up. If you were a little more deliberate or maybe struggling a bit, he would take you out of your game.

I started making it a point to get to the cart first and set up to drive. I frequently tipped the club boy, whispering instructions to make sure he had me on the driver's side. It worked like clockwork. It fucked with M.J.'s tempo. It was subtle, but think about it. I could take a little bit of his edge by intervening with his tempo. Athletes understand that and golfers understand that.

I remember a couple of occasions when M.J. insisted on driving.

"Fine," I said. "I'll drive the other cart."

Later, M.J. would insist on his own cart, because, I think, of his need to develop a sense of control of his game.

I would drive the other cart and dilly-dally around trying to control the tempo anyway.

Was it fair? Of course. I've never heard of a 24-second clock in golf. What's more, even at my tactical pace, the groups ahead were always moving aside to let us play through. I will concede that they could well have been doing that so they could watch Michael Jordan.

━━━━━

I got my butt kicked at Stardust that first morning. M.J. got me all five ways for $2,500. I read later, I think in Golf Digest, that he had shot his career round.

According to my recollection, Michael shot a 74. Ron Heitzinger, our nut with numbers and rounds, remembered it as a 34-39=73. Regardless, my 78 was good but not good enough.

The key, to me, was that 39 on the back. Ron, who walked along with us since he had lost the coin flip, remembered that M.J. shanked a few shots and let us back into the game. If he hadn't shanked a few, heaven knows what he might have shot. The point was that he showed himself to be human, at least on a golf course.

It briefly crossed my mind that he might have been sand-bagging. That is the art of playing and negotiating well enough to win but not so well as to discourage defeated opponents from further competition. If that had been the case, we would have been in trouble. It wasn't.

As would become typical of our days on the golf course, we had already decided we would play an afternoon round before we had finished the one in the morning. Eventually, we just scheduled morning and afternoon rounds.

Ernie Banks isn't the only Chicago guy whose motto was "Let's play two." Only with Jordan it was rounds of golf rather than baseball.

"That was one of the most difficult things about playing with Jordan," Eric Weinberg recalled. "It was a given with him. You were playing with him, you went 36 holes. He was going to play until the sun went down, period. And the second round was hardly ever on the same course."

We covered 36 holes on probably 80 per cent of our golfing days. Exercise nuts might try playing 36 holes of intense golf daily for seven straight days and see how they feel.

"I'll tell you," Eric said, "everyone's scores went up dramatically in those second rounds. It became a matter of survival."

I was able to help myself by calling upon the benefits of transcendental-meditation and yoga to keep myself together. I don't recall that my scores went up that dramatically in the afternoon rounds, but Eric might have been right about all of our scores being a little higher.

■

After that first morning round, Jordan excused himself briefly.

"I have to make a very important telephone call," he said.

I later heard he had called to cancel an appearance on the Arsenio Hall Show. Even President Bush would learn that golf has a rather high priority in Jordan's life away from basketball.

In a sense, our escapade was out of control from its inception, at least in terms of one of us blowing off an important engagement. I would learn that blowing off social or professional obligations was one of the benchmarks of the compulsive or addicted gambler. I concede that I would occasionally alter social obligations, but I never sacrificed professional responsibilities.

For the afternoon round, we headed north up Interstate-15 to Carmel Mountain in the bedroom community of Rancho Penasquitos. I have always despised Carmel Mountain. It's one of those courses which winds through a cookie-cutter subdivision. The distances from some of the greens to the next tees would be like $20 taxi rides. It's ridiculous.

We had another very competitive round. I don't recall what we shot, but I do recall that Jordan beat me again. I think I dropped a couple thousand more. Ron played at Carmel

Mountain and he dropped a little bit too, though even then the others in my group were playing for less than I was.

"My range," Heitzinger told me, "was win or lose $300 or $400. It was possible I could have won or lost $1,000 or $2,000 if one of us played real well and the other played real badly. Generally, though, what I won or lost with Michael was tip money to him."

Ron knew his numbers. Freddy didn't think they mattered when it came down to the competition itself.

"I don't know what you and Jordan might have been playing for," Freddy told me, "but I sensed he wanted to beat me for my $300 or whatever just as badly. I think the competition stimulated him more than the money."

———

Before Michael left town, he asked if I would play in a tournament benefiting the United Negro College Fund at La Costa Resort and Spa a few weeks later. Of course I agreed. I was flattered. I felt our first taste of competition had already forged a friendship.

What he didn't tell me, or the world for that matter, was that he was about to get married. After he arrived in San Diego, he told us that he and his girlfriend, the former Juanita Vanoy, had been married a few days before in Las Vegas. We all felt we were sort of privy to a scoop. We hadn't yet heard the news, because it hadn't been on the news.

La Costa, it turned out, happened to be a perfect place for a honeymoon.

Naturally, Michael broke this news to us on the golf course. Days would always be his, which meant he would play golf, and evenings would always be Juanita's. This was the way it always was when Juanita accompanied him and that was fine. We were all family men with family values we always kept in perspective.

We played 72 holes in two days before M.J.'s tournament, 36 at Stardust and 36 at The Farms, according to Heitzinger's meticulous records. I tapped him good this time. I came out $7,000 ahead. Later, when we realized it was silly to write checks after every round, we would run what amounted to tabs on one another's debt. The tabs would go up and down, first one ahead and then the other. One of us would get a lead and the other would cancel it out. In our standings, "games behind" came with dollar signs. But we didn't start running our tab until 1990.

On this day at La Costa, I would get a check for $7,000. I actually got it on the course, and I wasn't even in Jordan's group. This was the only time we ever played in separate groups. The biggest contributors, corporate guys, got to play with the big guy. The others just got to see him on the course and rub shoulders at a dinner and tell the members back at their clubs how close they had been to a legend.

When our paths crossed during the round of golf, M.J. slipped me a check for the $7,000. I thought it ironic how some high rollers had paid some outrageous amounts to play 18 holes with Michael and here I was pocketing a personal check for seven grand.

Michael Jordan signed a lot of autographs that day, but I liked the one I got best.

The one on the lower right corner of that check.

———

Later in the summer of 1989, not too long before Michael had to report to training camp with the Chicago Bulls, I accepted an invitation to visit him at his home in Hilton Head, S.C.

One of his homeboys picked me up at the airport. He had these buddies, No. 1 being that fellow Adolph Shiver, who hung with him. There were also three Freds. I just called them The Freds. One was Whitfield, another Kearns and a third whose last name I cannot recall.

One of the Freds came and got me and took me to Jordan's home. It looked like something off a plantation, worth at least half a million and probably more. It wasn't bad for a second home.

M.J. employed this large, affable black woman who reminded me of Aunt Jemima. She took care of us, cooking our meals and doing our laundry. She treated us like we were extended family.

If there was any daylight at all, we were playing golf. If it was dark, we were playing cards. During one of the card games, Adolph and one of the Freds got into an embarrassing argument and Michael had to pull them apart. It was classic Adolph... too much lip movement.

Meanwhile, I was getting beaten up at both golf and cards.

The card game was something called Tonk. It's an urban game. I can never seem to remember the rules until I sit down and play a hand or two. I'd first played it back in the caddy shack in Columbus.

I didn't like to lose at cards and I hated to lose at golf. I have never learned how to deal with losing, with the empty sensation it creates in my gut. My body undergoes a chemical transformation it takes hours to shake. The amount of the loss is not as important as the feeling of having lost.

Our multi-day match came down to the last hole on the last day. I had a 70-foot putt, a big money putt over a green with a lot of undulations. It was very tricky, very treacherous. All I had to do was get down in two to win or three to tie. The swing was winning $12,000 or losing $6,000.

I like big pressure and I'm a competitive guy, but my hands were shaking and I was sweating. I had a case of the nerves. A bad case. It was nothing like what would come later, but rather a first taste. This experience prompted me to alter the grip on my putter, wrapping it with gauze to absorb the sweat and give me a tighter grip with better control.

I wanted to kick the world's greatest athlete's ass for all his homeboys to watch. He wasn't saying much, but I think he was getting off on the pressure.

Jordan had his posse there, Adolph and The Freds. I once heard Charles Barkley say that Adolph was M.J.'s boy, much like the image of a prisoner being another prisoner's boy. Adolph is always running off at the mouth, kind of like Barkley in the press, and being a nuisance and a distraction. Michael wouldn't talk trash on the course, but Adolph would do it for him...like a good boy would.

I took four putts to get the damned ball in the hole. I was just devastated. I never take four putts. I can't recall when I might have done that before or since. I pride myself in being cool under the heat and this was embarrassing.

"E-Man, I don't like to win that way," M.J. told me.

"Michael, I don't like to lose that way," I said.

I wrote a check for $6,500. I had lost at cards too. It was an expensive trip, but I tipped Aunt Jemima nicely for taking such good care of us.

We had started a roller-coaster ride with incredible lows and exhilarating highs.

Chapter Four

The Arena

New York City was good to me. I was raised in the West Virginia hills and a Columbus slum and now, though I wasn't exactly a wheel, I was wheeling and dealing in the biggest jungle on earth.

I had to translate my Ohio State book smarts to 57th and Broadway street smarts. The pace was hot and I loved it.

I was learning this hotshot slick marketing stuff, the state-of-the-art stuff. In New York, you better absorb and assimilate because you're around talented people and the pressure is always on. If you can't keep up, you better get the hell out.

Taking my hayseed background to New York had been another one of my gambles, but I had the energy and the confidence and talent to keep up with the pressure cooker.

After I had been in New York City for awhile, I started needing more of a challenge than my small agency. I had heard of Harry Cooper and his work with academic data banks. I was working with a data base associated with both athletics and academics. I could see a mesh which might work.

I had targeted three or four companies I wanted to approach, but Harry's Career Guidance Foundation was the most interesting. I called Harry at his home near San Diego, California.

Harry was impressed with my knowledge of computers and data bases, and he didn't figure to be easy to impress. He was ahead of his time when it came to computers and the power they possessed. He had made his money in New York, so he checked me out with contacts there and concluded I was a solid citizen and an up-and-coming young guy.

I was on my way to San Diego for an interview.

———

Harry's niece, Kerry Cooper, was basically president of the Career Guidance Foundation without the title. She had been going to college at Georgia State in Atlanta when her uncle called and told her what he was doing in San Diego with the CGF and asked if she would like to be a part of it.

"Sure, Uncle Harry," she said, "I can type your letters or do your filing or whatever you want."

"Kerry," her uncle said, "I can go out into the street here and hire a secretary. I want you to run the place."

And so she did. The Career Guidance Foundation is a micro-publisher with maybe 3,600 college catalogues on micro-fiche. You can save forests by putting college catalogues on micro-fiche and getting them to college admission offices, libraries and high schools in that form. That's what Harry and Kerry were doing.

However, as Kerry would explain it to me later, the timing of my approach was perfect. The CGF was a little dead in the water because the director of marketing had gone a little stale on the job. They were looking for fresh blood, a new approach.

And there I was, knocking at the door with my New York City sizzle.

If I sound arrogant and cocky, it's probably because I was.

Kerry would tell you that. In fact, I think I'll let her...

I was living with Uncle Harry when this guy
called and started talking about his athletic

scholarship data base. He sent this brochure all marked up with ideas on how to market our collection.

"Would you look at this?" I asked Uncle Harry. "Who does this guy think he is?"

I thought to myself, "Oh God, just what we need is some guy like this."

My Uncle Harry is one of those visionaries. That's what got him where he was. He always has real good ideas, even though some of them seem way out there at the time. He asked me to call this guy Richard Esquinas and send him a ticket. He wanted him to come out for a weekend for an interview.

I was thinking, "This will be the answer to my marketing problem?"

I was so excited at the prospect that I didn't bother to cancel the weekend I had planned in Los Angeles. I only met Richard briefly, like 20 minutes in the office. He was wearing a plaid tie and a powder blue jacket. I was laughing inside. I thought he might be alright if he got rid of the tie and the jacket. He was just so cocky.

Harry hired him that weekend. He never did things like that. Never. We had these phone conversations before he came out, batting ideas back and forth. Then he got here and I had to deal with him. And I had the political problem of moving the old guy out and moving Rich in.

I thought we had been doing fine, not great, and then Rich came in as this bigger than life kind of person with all these state-of-the-art ideas. I'm more genteel, sensitive to people's feelings, but Rich just came barreling in and said change this and change that.

We were at each other's throats all the time. I later had to admit they were good ideas.

—

I married Kerry. My therapist, Lori Stephenson, didn't know who Kerry was until I had had a few sessions. She shook her head.

"You not only married the big boss's niece, who was almost a daughter to him," she said, "but you married your own boss, your direct superior. You just don't do that sort of thing."

She knew me by then.

"Never mind," Lori said,. "You do. But that was another big risk."

Marrying her may not have been as big a risk as having the nerve to court her. Harry and I had a business relationship which gave me a lot of latitude, but I wasn't sure if courting his niece was part of it.

Kerry broke a couple of dinner "dates," which I viewed more as opportunities to go over business in a relaxed atmosphere. I think I had dates in mind without coming out and asking. Something would always come up and she would either cancel or just not show.

Finally, she invited me to a birthday party for one of her friends, just to give the new guy at the office a chance to meet some people. We ended up playing backgammon for the whole party, then went home and sat up all night telling each other our secrets.

One secret I didn't tell her was that I liked to gamble. She learned that later.

—

In truth, I had not seen pursuing Kerry as a gamble. It had not occurred to me that it might have negatively impacted our business relationship had she not been interested, which seemed for awhile to be the case. And I hadn't thought about the potential for negatively impacting my relationship with her uncle.

As Kerry said, I just had a tendency to barrel into things assuming they would work out. I barreled into this relationship with Kerry because she had everything a guy could want in a woman...looks, brains, warmth, humor, spunk.

She was raised in Mississippi and still has this Gone With the Wind accent.

I saw her as a refreshing breath of fresh air and I know she saw me the same way.

"Rich was totally different," she told a friend. "He was real and honest. Most guys in Southern California are totally superficial. They all seem to be in investments or real estate. They're like plastic surgeons' dreams."

She took me to Disneyland, of all places, and then to a movie. We saw "E.T." We were together from then on, though we stayed in the closet for awhile because of our business relationship. We finally showed up together for a family dinner at Mr. A's restaurant.

Harry Cooper pulled us aside the next day with a warning: "I hope you two know what you are doing."

We did. We met in 1982 and were married in 1983. We have been together since and have a beautiful daughter named Felicity.

If that was a gamble, it was the smartest one of my life.

———

After I came in with my marketing skills, I was able to upgrade sales by 100 per cent after three or four years at the Career Guidance Foundation.

"You turn it around," Harry said, "and I'll be good to you."

One of the main things I had to change was image. I came in and all these young people were San Diego—casual with shorts and T-shirts. I was Manhattan. Not a day went by when I wasn't wearing a tie. Everyone wears them now.

It was, after all, a business. Part of my compensation was

that I was able to establish the Athletic Guidance Center (AGC). We helped high school kids find athletic scholarships and published the Academic Athletic Journal, an official publication of the National Collegiate Athletic Association. In fact, I was the first Executive Director of the National Association of Academic Advisers for Athletics (NAAA).

I enjoyed all of this work with academics, because they were missions with higher causes, if you will. God knows, I like higher causes.

Kerry and I had a strong household income, probably $150,000 to $180,000, when we were married, and more like $250,000 for the last seven or eight years. We reported close to $500,000 on our 1992 tax return, adding $125,000 in gambling gains from my golf with M.J. to our combined incomes. Our earnings have allowed us to own a nice home in a prime La Jolla location and fuel a nice lifestyle.

Things were going so well with our businesses through those earlier years that Harry's confidence in my decision-making and deal-making grew stronger. I learned a lot from watching Harry and his dealings with his prime real estate at the Interstate 5 and 805 junction in Sorrento Hills, one of San Diego's booming areas. He would share with me what he was thinking and talk numbers with me regarding detailed projects, this was an era where banks and savings and loans were running around putting mega bucks in southern California dirt. He was talking numbers beyond what I had experienced.

I was getting antsy for a new challenge, new stimulation, new risk. I was ready to bring my juices to a boil.

———

I heard rumbling that the San Diego Sports Arena was available in late 1988. This intrigued me. It was a whole new universe. It figured to be complicated and political and 25 hours a day worth of challenging.

Exactly what I had in mind. I took a proposal to Harry.

"We buy the Sports Arena," I said, "but not because we want the existing arena. We need San Diego's arena business for a greater cause. I've seen you bring all these deals in on your land. Why not a new sports arena? Why not control the whole process by having the existing arena?"

I proposed that we build a new state-of-the-art arena on Harry's land in the Sorrento Valley. We put together a marquee property and go after the National Basketball Association and the National Hockey League. We build a trophy facility for the community.

This automatically got Harry's mind churning. He thought it was a viable project. He had both the land and the mindset. Harry never guessed it would have been such a risk.

Harry was willing to gamble, and this was a major gamble. His land and his property were the collateral we used to make a classic 80's leveraged loan. We utilized a nonperforming asset, his land, the dirt at Interstates 5 and 805, to buy a performing asset, the Sports Arena.

The cost was $10 million, but we actually financed more to fuel operating expenses and potential losses.

When it came to taking risks, putting me with Harry was like putting kerosene on a fire.

It was a huge gamble.

I had received benefits, a 30 per cent equity piece which certainly bumped me up in terms of my own personal cash and equity position. That was Harry's generous compensation to me for putting the deal together. I later returned 15 per cent to Harry because I thought it was a fair and equitable way of treating his degree of risk in relation to mine.

Now I felt the pressure to run it. Nobody else could have felt it like I did, because I was his partner and I had put Harry at so much risk. It was a driving force for me. The day-to-day pressure kept me from distractions. Jordan and I might have played for months rather than days at a time if I had not been dedicated to my responsibilities at the Sports Arena.

I was a workaholic. I had an almost psycho perception of how hard I had to work to make this succeed. Harry wasn't out a lot of hard money but he had put $40 million worth of property at risk for this loan and this undertaking. That's forty fucking million. I put my arms around that building. There wasn't anything I was afraid to do. There wasn't anything I felt it was beneath me to do.

If I had been in search of a huge gamble to motivate me, I had one.

Compulsive behavior was overtaking me and impacting my domestic life. The only time I seemed to get home was to get my daughter to bed and grab dinner. Working ridiculous hours is a form of compulsive behavior society applauds, because hard work is the backbone of America, right? However, it sure wreaks havoc on the family unit, which is a more important backbone of America. Even positive compulsive behavior can have its negative side effects.

Kerry was understanding. Kerry had worked hard all her life to get what she had. She understood that her husband was working hard for the benefit of her and Felicity...and, of course, Uncle Harry.

———

When we called the press conference to announce our acquisition, we immediately made it clear that we had grand plans for the future.

Harry looked cool and dapper as usual, with his neatly trimmed moustache and dark hair. He might have been Clark Gable in another life. He was Mr. Debonair.

I was the young lion who did most of the roaring. Harry was

happy being more the background guy. He was happy making a brief statement and turning the microphone over to me.

Before the media packed the room, we had talked about the image we would project.

We were making first impressions.

Both of us had been in San Diego for awhile and both of us had been successful, none of the movers and shakers knew who we were. We were just two more guys driving nice cars and living nice lives. Guys like us were all over the landscape.

It was not quite like buying a professional sports franchise, but it would change our profile considerably. We were the new owners of the San Diego Sports Arena. More precisely, we owned the lease from the city to operate that arena, and it was almost the same thing as owning it. We would call the shots.

Suddenly, Harry Cooper and Rich Esquinas were news, all over the front pages of newspapers and major faces on the 11 o'clock news. We were just like any other Tom, Rich or Harry before that press conference.

Our ace in the hole, our attention-getter, was our splash about our future plans. We had no hidden agenda, this desire to use the old arena as a stepping stone to a new one. We wanted that right out front. We wanted it known that we were there to make a difference for the community.

We would upgrade the existing arena. We would pursue a tenant from the NBA. We would pursue a tenant from the NHL. We would build a new arena on Harry's land in the Sorrento Valley.

We would leave monuments to our stewardship. Both the San Diego *Union* and San Diego *Tribune* reported our acquisition on the front page...not the sports page.

"Building Gets New Lease on Life," said the *Tribune* headline.

"New Owners to Replace Facility With Bigger One," said the *Union* headline.

It was far from a one-day phenomenon. The *Tribune*

followed with another headline which captured the pulse of the community: "Plans for New Arena Stirring City's Dreams... Enthusiasm Mounts for a New Facility That Might House NBA, NHL Franchises."

Tom Cushman, then the *Tribune* sports editor and now the *Union-Tribune* sports editor, wrote: "In a sequence so dazzling those exposed were left with sunburned eyeballs, the two purchased the existing lease to the Sports Arena, recommended a dust-to-dust fate for the building and announced plans to erect a 22,000-seat replacement somewhere within the city limits."

Another writer likened us to Butch Cassidy and the Sundance Kid riding out of the La Jolla hills.

One newspaper reporter told me that our story was the most reported local story of 1989. I don't know what he used as a measuring stick, but two very private, very low-profile guys were suddenly very public.

We were fresh new faces on the landscape. We were out of the background and into the limelight. We were also into a snakepit.

■■■■

San Diego had not had much luck getting and retaining professional sports teams in the Sports Arena. Two different NBA teams had fled, the Rockets to Houston and the Clippers to Los Angeles, and the American Basketball Association died in San Diego before it died everywhere else. The NHL had never been in San Diego, but the World Hockey Association came to San Diego and went the way of the ABA.

Indoor sports seemed cursed in San Diego, perhaps the most quintessential outdoor town. Part of it was bad luck with ownership, part bad luck with leagues and part bad luck with a facility which had not been maintained at a major league level.

Harry and I were convinced that San Diego would support

both the NBA and NHL. After all, the metropolitan area is like the seventh largest in the nation. We were prepared to upgrade the existing facility so it would be an appropriate temporary venue while we were going through the machinations to build a state-of-the-art facility.

Our game plan was never to actually own a professional franchise. Those are toys for the richest of men. We had money, but we weren't exactly Forbes 500 candidates. We knew we didn't have the cash to own a franchise, but we had the formula and we owned the property.

Our job was one of enlightenment. We had to enlighten the community and get it behind us and we had to enlighten the NBA and the NHL and get them interested in the community. Given the right circumstances, which we felt we could put in place, franchises would thrive in San Diego.

To get franchises, we had to lure existing teams which were disgruntled with their current situations or schmooze league hierarchy for expansion teams. We went both directions.

Donald Sterling was a help to us. He is persona non grata in San Diego, because he made the decision to move the Clippers to Los Angeles after the 1983-84 season. He took a lot of heat because of the community's perception that he was looking for almost any excuse to get his team closer to his Beverly Hills home. Disappointing teams produced disappointing attendance and gave him his out.

In talking to Don, I came to understand that problems with the previous arena ownership were a big part of his departure. There were unique issues involving repairs and improvements of the facility which were apparently far from adequately addressed. He told several people that the Clippers would never have left San Diego if Cooper and Esquinas owned the arena at the time. He publicly said we were great for the building and complimented how we ran the building.

The first time we had dinner with Don we were talking about San Diego and he was saying nice things and I asked him if he would ever be interested in selling to someone who might bring the Clippers back. I unintentionally offended him.

"Rich," he said, "I don't know that I'd ever sell the Clippers, period."

He obviously forgave me my insensitive suggestion. I have nothing but nice things to say about Don Sterling. I always saw him as an ally, a player on our side. He was pro-San Diego in support of our lobbying efforts. We met with him for occasional dinners and talked shop and he gave us behind-the-scenes looks at what was happening in the NBA. He introduced us to key players and talked highly of Harry and me and San Diego.

Nothing could be done about milk spilled in the past, but Don was doing everything he could to help us with the future. To this day, I like and respect Don.

Another of those key players we met was Barry Ackerly, the owner of the Seattle Supersonics. He was in the midst of frustrating negotiations with the city and he was looking in other directions. We were hopeful we could work something out.

We went back and forth with Barry, discussing a potential move. At one time, we had very substantive conversations. We knew there was a risk that maybe he was using us as a tool back in Seattle, but that was part of the games we had to play. We owed it to San Diego, and ourselves, to pursue whatever possibilities presented themselves.

As it turned out, Barry worked things out in Seattle and the Supersonics stayed put. We had had a nice but unfulfilled flirtation with a very solid franchise.

Jerry Buss, who owns the Lakers and the Forum in Los Angeles, was also helpful. He was one of the players we were bidding against when we went after the arena. He has a home in San Diego and an interest in the area. We just outbid him, plus our plans for a new arena cast a tall shadow.

Jerry's one of the most high-powered men in the country when it comes to sports and entertainment and we talked shop maybe a half-dozen times, picking his brain and looking for ideas. I never bothered to ask him about moving the Lakers to San Diego, because I knew that would be a ridiculous notion. Jerry, like Sterling, was wired with the NBA as well as the NHL, that coming from his days as owner of the Los Angeles Kings. He also gave me guidance when it came to boxing and entertainment, two staples in our venue.

At one point, a few years later, Jerry paid me the highest personal compliment I have ever been paid. He told the group negotiating to buy the arena from Harry and me that I should always be a part of the mix because I was one of the finest general managers in the country.

When I brought Muhammad Ali to San Diego for one of Terry Norris's title fights, I sat he and Jerry Buss together ringside. In their own individual ways, those guys packed one helluva lot of clout.

I had met Ali at a private gathering at a home on Mount Helix, an area of nice homes in the eastern part of San Diego. It had to do with a tie-in between Sprint and Ali's foundation.

As we were visiting, I invited him to come out, at my expense, for the Norris fight. He accepted, though I thought he was just being agreeable. One of his representatives called me and said he intended to fulfill his commitment.

I was thrilled. I had Ali and Ken Norton, two boxing greats, at a pre-fight party and I presented them with posters to commemorate a great fight they had had at the Sports Arena 20 years earlier.

"Well, Rich," Ali said in that style which has grown so deliberate, "I come all the way from Chicago and all I get is a poster?"

"Ali," I said, "I didn't know what else to give a man like you."

■■■

When it came to attracting an NBA franchise, we kept schmoozing and we kept losing.

We decided to approach the NHL from a slightly different direction. We did the usual exercises, such as making presentations at league meetings, but we took it a step further. We thought we would acquire a minor league team, which was within our financial means, and use it as a stepping stone.

Nothing shows credibility and sincerity quite like actually having a franchise or at least a game in the venue. That was our reasoning when we fronted the money for that original NBA All-Star game and the others which followed on an annual basis.

Early in 1990, probably January or February, we became aware that an International Hockey League franchise was available. We felt that purchasing an IHL team would wave our flag and illustrate how serious we were. It would give us a chance to start nurturing and stimulating the hockey market in San Diego.

Once again, we were gambling. Once again, Harry's assets were going to be stressed.

We had put $750,000 of our earnings into new arena development and now we paid an additional $250,000 to the IHL as a franchise fee for the privilege of losing another $1 million. But we were committed to getting the team we would call the Gulls up and skating.

Harry was, as usual, in a go-for-it mode. I had suggested to him at one point that maybe he should sell his land, which would have gotten him $22 million, and consolidate his assets. A later offer was down to $14 million, so he was reticent to take the money and run. He could be daring, but he was also patient.

We would fund the Gulls from within the Sports Arena's financial superstructure, meaning with earnings. Obviously, these were earnings which might otherwise have been pocketed.

To be credible in our pursuit, we felt we had to have hockey. To make our proposed new arena work, we absolutely had to have an anchor tenant from either the NBA or the NHL. This was our gesture to the NHL...and to the community. San Diego had always been supportive of minor league hockey, including the Gulls in a previous incarnation.

Our plan in purchasing the IHL franchise, which came from Flint, Michigan, was that we would keep it in San Diego until the NHL arrived and then move it to Fresno or Las Vegas and have it function as a farm team for our major league franchise.

We hired Don Waddell, a solid hockey guy with a solid background, to put the team itself together. We did not have an affiliation with an NHL team, so Don had to scrape together whatever players he could get from wherever he could get them.

I was co-owner the first year with Harry, of course, and stepped in as president for the 1991-92 season. I followed hockey as a kid and knew a little bit about the sport, but I was more attuned to the operations end, such as building the ice and setting up the arena and prepping the ice. I was hands-on in all areas where I had expertise, such as cutting a radio deal.

Obviously, I wasn't the hockey guy. Don Waddell was the hockey guy. I discussed things such as player contracts and budgets and marketing with him, but I didn't know anything about the players themselves. Don knows every fricking guy who has ever put on a pair of skates and he has a strong network in terms of how to get them. Putting the team together was his chore.

Fred Comrie, owner of a large furniture chain in San Diego, bought the Gulls from us during the 1992 season. I still feel good about the role I had in bringing them to town. I feel very proud that the 1993 Gulls won 62 games during the regular season, more than any other professional team in hockey history.

Our baby had grown up to be a beautiful child.

———

Remember how the guys in my regular golf group called ourselves Closed Shop because we rarely engaged with outsiders?

I didn't appreciate what a closed shop really was until I started butting heads with the San Diego political leadership.

After we announced our goals for the arena, virtually every politician and money player in town went out of his or her way to wine and dine and become familiar with Harry Cooper and Richard Esquinas. We had caught them off-guard. We had come from outside their loop and acquired a marquee San Diego facility.

As a co-owner at a very young age, I was intentionally overly-humble in these dealings with the shakers and movers. I took great pains to show respect, almost to a fault. I thought that after awhile, given that I had some power in the San Diego sportscene, I would get respect in return. For example, I thought that the Greater San Diego Sports Association, a civic group, should be nurturing a plan for young people to take over the passing of the baton. I was a player in the community, but I never got that feeling from most of the gurus. If I wasn't being groomed to become part of leadership, who in hell was? A lot of young, up-and-coming bucks felt the same way. It was a very parochial setting.

We were mixing, trying to blend with all the right people. We met with power brokers from every sector imaginable, people who really influence the economy. We met with the media, such as the Copley press and radio stations. We met with other franchise owners in town, such as the Padres and Chargers, even though they weren't arena tenants. We met with every politician, even backed a lot of them financially in their election campaigns.

I started to feel resentment and animosity toward me, being a young guy getting newfound attention because I was part of a high-profile project with such potential for excitement in the community. I had the audacity to take aim at changing and updating and flushing out many of the structural things going on with the power in San Diego. I was beginning to feel I was trying to mix in circles that didn't want me or what I represented...change.

I was starting to feel an edge to these encounters, an edge which paralleled in a way the feeling of being on the first tee with Michael Jordan in a big money game.

From the very beginning, the one politician with whom we got nowhere was the mayor. Our relationship with the mayor, Maureen O'Connor, was strained from the beginning. We had come out of nowhere with this specific plan for a very worthwhile project for the community and we got no response from O'Connor.

The mayor's leadership in this area was so weak it was appalling. She wouldn't shoulder the responsibility of taking a lead on what would be a dynamic project. You look at other cities seeking franchises or trying to build new venues and you see they are always very dependent on leadership from the local governments, particularly the mayor.

We were flabbergasted. On several occasions we attempted to meet with Maureen O'Connor, but we were told she would not meet us because she did not want to be aligned with a controversial project. It's really great when the mayor will only align herself when everyone else is also in agreement. That's bullshit leadership.

I have to laugh a bittersweet laugh at O'Connor's refusal to meet with us. The telephone rang in my office one day and it was the mayor's office. Janet Jackson was appearing in concert at the Sports Arena and the mayor wanted us to arrange a meeting between her and the star.

Here I was, frustrated over months of trying to meet with the mayor, and now I had to go through the protocol and maneuvers with Janet Jackson's people so that our apparently star-struck mayor could blow smoke up a superstar's ass in our facility.

Maureen O'Connor got her meeting with Janet Jackson, but we never got our meeting with Maureen O'Conner.

━━━

If our project had become controversial, which it had, it was because the ugliness of greed had crawled into the picture like some slimy monster. It came from the private sector and it came from the political sector.

Harry's idea, and my idea, was to put the new facility on his land in the northern part of the city. This was the sensible location, in more ways than one. The land was already in place, already in possession of one of the project's principals. That should almost have been enough. But there was more. San Diego's booming growth was to the north, making such a location geographically perfect. What's more, three major freeways were on the doorstep to Harry's property and three others were nearby, making for smooth access and egress to events.

What was shaking with the shakers and movers? The powers-that-be wanted the project in downtown San Diego, far from the population base and totally inaccessible to major freeways except through already congested downtown streets. Now they occupied their time debating which downtown location was most appropriate, probably meaning which downtown location would be most lucrative to which shaker and mover. Meanwhile, we had to fund the development cost as these whims blew like clouds in the wind.

Our little dream, the dream of two gamblers from outside the loop, was as outside the loop as we had been from the beginning.

As far as the NBA and NHL were concerned, we were at a loss as to how to possibly present a united effort from San Diego when we couldn't even get the united support of San Diego's leaders.

Harry and I would ultimately sell 50 per cent of the arena, plus an option on the remaining 50 per cent, to a local group we perceived to be politically correct in local circles. We had opened the window and brought legitimacy to a community yearning for such a project, but this window of opportunity may have gotten around the financial curve.

Now Anaheim, of all places, has an NHL franchise and San Diego does not have a franchise of any kind in either of the two major indoor sports.

I remain a strong advocate of franchises in San Diego, but I fear it will be a long time before the NHL or NBA take a serious look at one of America's otherwise finest cities. It could be a tough project with the window we opened coming to a close.

Chapter Five

The Golfer

It may come as a surprise that my La Jolla home does not back up to a golf course. You'd think I would want to wander out the back door and step onto a fairway. A bighorn sheep could not play the "fairway" behind my house.

I have a multi-level deck looking down on one of those canyons which run like arteries through San Diego and isolate so many distinctive neighborhoods. My house is in the high-rent district near the top of Mount Soledad. It was a steal when Kerry and I bought it 10 years ago and it's probably worth over $700,000 now, even in a depressed market.

All of the underbrush and trees in the canyon conceal a secret it shares only with me.

It is full of golf balls. Thousands of them. I buy used golf balls by the box from a driving range wholesaler. I don't mean by the dozen either. I mean by the box, like the size box you grab from behind the market when you are packing grandma's china for a move. These are decent balls retrieved from ponds and water hazards, not that it makes much difference. All I am going to do with them is pound them off my deck and into the canyon.

My canyon is my driving range. I don't worry about rattle-snakes slithering up into my yard, because I don't think they can withstand the bombardment. That canyon is a rattlesnake's Baghdad.

Actor Jack Nicholson has the same kind of backyard driving range, probably because of privacy more than convenience. I read about it somewhere and then had an opportunity to ask him about it when M.J. and I ran into him during a round at Hillcrest in L.A.

If I tire of pounding golf balls, I can putt them on an artificial surface along the south side of the house. I haven't found a putting green quite as fast as my practice green. I haven't found any as flat either, but it does assimilate a putting surface.

Obviously, I like to work on my golf game. I like to hone it and sharpen it. When I get into periods when I am too busy to play, I can keep an edge with my backyard practice. It's easier being the workaholic I am just to step out my back door and flail away. Another nice benefit is that my daughter can be with me, working on following her daddy's footsteps at the age of six.

▬▬▬

With help from Jack Nicklaus, I taught myself how to play golf.   Jack didn't personally coach me, of course, but I think I have read everything he has written about the game. It started when I was a kid, reading his tips in the Columbus *Dispatch* newspaper, and it continues to this day.

Naturally, I got interested in golf when I was caddying at Winding Hollow Country Club in Columbus. It was impossible to haul all those clubs without getting interested, especially since caddies could play for free one morning a week.

I had only caddied for about a month before I went out and bought myself a beginner's set of Northwestern clubs for $49. I probably pay twice that per club now. There was a driving range across from Winding Hollow and I'd stop and hit balls before going home.

I hit balls out of my backyard in Columbus too. The house backed up to a vacant lot and I'd hit wedges at the telephone poles. I developed a good short game because I spent so much time hitting half wedges, three-quarter wedges and full wedges into that vacant lot. Needless to say, I retrieved those balls.

Putting? I did that in the kitchen. I practiced 10-footers, using the heating vent on the floor as my hole.

I never took lessons in my formative years. I never had that kind of grooming, partially because I couldn't afford the investment.

When I could afford lessons, I was a demanding student. I pushed the pros to be as good as they could be so that I could be as good as I could be.

In between lessons, and even now it's rare when I take a lesson, I make my own adjustments. I pick up tidbits here and there from playing with good golfers as well. And I have kept on reading. I could be a poster boy for *Golf Digest*.

———

The one area which is most characteristic of my game has nothing to do with driving or chipping or putting.

It's not physical. It's mental. When I would get into a downward slide on the course, Jordan frequently would tell me and our group that he knew I would never give up or give in. The mental toughness and determination which held me in such good stead in life was also my ally on the golf course.

I know it's a cliche, but I got tougher in the toughest situations.

Put me in a tough spot on a golf course and I could escape. My driver's erratic so I have to make great recovery shots to play well. I think I could get out of a jail with my short game. My fellow Spaniard Seve Ballesteros is my hero in this regard.

Like Seve, I would rather go daring than conservative when I am trying to get out of trouble.

"If my driver's on," I once told M.J., "you're gonna lose. I'm too long for you."

It was as simple as that. He knew it too, even though he can hardly be described as a Punch-and-Judy hitter off the tee. If my driver's on and I'm in the fairway, I'll be flipping in wedges where everyone else is hitting six, seven and eight irons. There's a lot of difference between coming into a green with a wedge or a seven iron. You're going to make a lot more birdies with a wedge. You're going to bring a lot of holes to their knees.

I have this Freudian relationship with my driver, which can be so good or so bad depending on its mood. That year when our group broke down all the statistics and put them into a computer was typical for me. I was dead last in hitting fairways, but first in birdies, eagles and greens in regulation. My driver didn't always get me where I wanted to go, but it got me a long way from the tee.

"You're a little erratic," Eric Weinberg told me, "but you're always long and mean."

Long drivers get a certain respect because of the distance they bring to their games and what that distance brings to the shots which follow. I think the most glorious shot in golf is the drive, no matter the emphasis everyone attaches to putting. The best shot to watch, the most satisfying to hit, is the long drive. It's the sound, it's the feeling, it's everything.

I used to love it when shit-talking Ron Heitzinger would hit one big off the tee and gloat about it.

"You think that's such a big shot," I'd zing him, "how about you giving me 3-1 odds on a hefty wager I can't hit it past you?"

Nine times out of 10 he would slink off the tee without saying a word.

I don't know how many people have told me I should harness my driver, get it under control. They tell me I don't need this sci-fi driver, just an average drive that gets me out into the fairway with the average player. Let my irons do it from there. That's just not me. It comes back to the risk thing, the gambling thing. I'd rather get the big reward for the big drive and live with the risk.

M.J. and I would frequently get into driving contests. We liked the machismo of the long drive. The big drive certainly plays to the bravado of the gambler.

I'd hit a drive and say, "Come on, M.J. I'll go $100 you can't beat it." Later, it might be $1,000 rather than $100. Unlike Ron, Michael would usually rise to the challenge.

"You're on, E-Man," he would say.

He could drive a long way, but he couldn't drive with me if I was on. One of our rules, of course, was that the ball had to be on the fairway. He'd hit one long and straight and I'd tell him I'd match it, but he'd have to give me 3-1 odds.

It all gets back to the sensation of the big hit. We both liked it. Even the pros will admit there's nothing to match the majesty of a powerful drive. It's power.

We never bet much on the other stuff, like getting up and down out of traps. Once in awhile, if we were next to each other on the fringe of a green, we'd bet a unit—usually $1,000—on who would chip closest. The catch was that you had to make the putt. You had to get down in par.

The gambling part of golf was inbred in me almost from those days in the caddy shack. I really couldn't enjoy the game without it. It's the only way I know.

———

My buddy Freddy Sarno tells me that my golf game is a lot like me, a lot like my personality.

When I was thinking about writing this book, I was sitting back in my office with Fred just bullshitting. It was my 38th birthday and he had brought me one of the golf shirts he manufactures as a present.

"Fred," I said, "you probably know me and my game better than anybody. If you had to describe it, what would you say?"

"Rich," he said, "you're fiery and volatile and so is your golf game. When you're bad, you're really bad. When you're on, you're pretty amazing."

He pumped me up on my driving, and you know how I feel about that.

"You're longer than the average guy on the PGA Tour," he said. "You can hit some tremendous drives. I don't know where you get it from."

And Freddy really knew how to flatter a gambler.

"Aside from your driving," he said, "the thing that best characterizes your approach to golf is that you play aggressively no matter what the bet is and no matter what the odds against the shot. You never play the safe, conservative shot. You play balls to the wall."

Words like those were the nicest birthday presents he could have given me.

———

The mental part is so important in golf that my buddies and I hired a golf psychologist at one time. It was probably 1987 or 1988. We were all looking for an advantage, not necessarily against each other, but adding an edge on our games.

This guy came out for the day and gave us a seminar, played a round of golf with us. We'd talk situations. It was a mental exercise.

We were into what we thought were high-pressure, high-stakes games, though they were nickel-and-dime in relation to what Jordan and I got into. We wanted help learning how to control our thoughts and stay focused on the game.

I had had many situations where the bet had taken over. I was worrying about the bet rather than playing golf. You can't be tentative. That'll get you a shank or a duck hook or a bail-out to the right. You have to overcome the stress and control the decision to pull the trigger.

The mental stress of worrying about money vs. making a good shot preys on every golfer who gets into high stakes games. He taught us to settle into a shot, block outside stimuli and smoothly execute the swing. It certainly helped me when I teed it up with M.J., though not as much as my lifetime of TM and yoga.

———

All of this talk about money and the mental side of golf gets me to what I call the comfort zone. If you're a gambler on a golf course, it's an advantage to get your opponent out of his comfort zone.

Every golfer has a comfort zone. Some guys can play rounds for $100,000 and they're not out of their comfort zones because they are worth maybe $50 million. Other guys are out of their comfort zones with $10 bets.

You find people's comfort zones and then you have them. That's the edge. You get their minds off their games. You can accomplish that on the very first tee, depending on the success of your negotiations. You can challenge them to stakes beyond their reasonable level of play.

The comfort zone, by my definition, relates to what you can afford to lose without impacting your bank account or lifestyle. It can even be what you can afford to lose and still have discretionary money to go to the movies.

I'm not sure where Michael Jordan might get out of his comfort zone. He frequently talked to me about his great wealth, especially when we got into our highest levels of gambling, and he always talked of what he could afford to lose in relation to what I could afford to lose. Losing more than a million bucks may not have taken him out of his comfort zone, but I was concerned that he really couldn't afford to engage at such levels.

Regardless, compulsive gamblers will get out of their comfort zones. They cannot help themselves. It's getting out of their comfort zones that gives them the rush they seek. The rush they crave hooks them at monetary levels beyond their means.

Personally speaking, I got there with Michael Jordan. I once got so far beyond my comfort zone I couldn't see it with the Palomar telescope.

———

A key point to me was that all of the golf and all of the gambling had little or no impact on my work at the Sports Arena. I concede there might have been times when I left early or arrived late, but my routine of working 16 hours a day kept me from feeling guilty.

It was never like I was hanging around down at the building waiting for a golf game to happen.

During my hands-on time at the Sports Arena, I never, never sacrificed my work or my work ethic for golf. If anything, what I did sacrifice was the golf I could have had. I could have spent an entire summer with Jordan. I could have spent four summers with Jordan. I could have had so much golf and gambling it ain't funny. Maybe I am a workaholic first and a compulsive gambler second.

I never lost sight of the fact that my work was making everything happen in my life. My work allowed me to play the golf courses I was able to play. My work allowed me to travel to meet Jordan in places like Hilton Head and Chicago. My work allowed me to bet at the levels I was betting, until, of course, we got so far beyond sensible levels.

And I never lost sight of the fact that the Sports Arena deal was my gamble with Harry Cooper's money, as well as my equity. His land was lying there as collateral and my work ethic had to bail it out.

My regular group will tell you that the time I had to spend on the golf course dwindled significantly after I got into arena operations.

In truth, about the only time I played golf was when I knew I was getting together with Michael. I'd hit my driving range and get ready for him. I'd force the time I needed to hone my game out of what little time was my own.

When we played, I played as long as I could, as many days as I could, until my duties dragged me back to the arena.

———

M.J. and I both had our dietary quirks on the golf course, mine being a little more healthy. At least I think it was.

I got into this stuff I called brain food. It was powdery stuff called Focus. On the label, it was described as nutrients for the brain. It was a dietary supplement mixed with water. You know, designer food. Gucci food.

I would tote it around the golf course with me. Some stuff is for muscles and some for energy. This stuff was supposed to fuel what the brain needs, give it a charge, so to speak.

Jordan and I used to have this thing where he'd be eating candy bars and I'd be eating brain food.

He'd press me or challenge me on a drive or something and I'd haul out my brain food.

"You using that brain stuff again?" he'd say, and laugh.

He'd pull out a candy bar. He'd eat Hershey bars or Snickers or anything. He was a junk food dog.

I'd work on him psychologically.

"You can't beat me when I use this stuff," I'd say. "I can't believe the junk you're putting into your system."

I was mysterious about exactly what I was taking. I wanted him to be thinking about it and wondering about it. When I had success, I'd tell him he couldn't beat me when I had my Gucci food. We played games like that with each other's minds. What he was eating was no mystery and I wanted to plant negative thoughts about that.

Unfortunately, I first started using brain food on a golfing orgy through North Carolina in 1991. What happened to me on that trip was no testimony to all the wonderful things I told him brain food was going to do for my game. I'm surprised he didn't buy me a case of the stuff.

━━━━

From the time I first picked up a club during my days in the caddy shack, I wanted to be a professional golfer.

That was my dream. It seemed reasonable for awhile. I was second in my section in high school and that got me to the district tournament, where I shot an 81 in horrendous conditions. I chalked that up to a bad day in weather unconducive to good golf.

Then I got to West Hills, the community college in Coalinga, California, and played as the No. 1 guy on my team. Surely, I was on my way to the PGA Tour.

A major dash of reality smacked me when I got to Ohio State. My game wasn't quite fit enough to chase guys like John Cook to the bench. I might have given up too easily on making the Buckeye golf team, but I think I did the right thing in terms of prioritizing my education. I couldn't afford not to work and I couldn't afford to both work and play golf.

In hindsight, I wonder what might have happened if I'd had the money to invest in my education. That would have left me time to invest in golf. I've always had the thirst and the commitment.

I've even thought that now, at the age of 38 when I have the money to do different things, that maybe I could try to make it on the tour. I guess it sounds far-fetched, but I've always thought I could do better than I have.

My chances would be slim. I know that. Very slim. But what if I went through the exercise of honing my game for a year and getting the best of coaching and getting into shape for the qualifying school? It would be like living a fantasy, living out a dream that I always wanted to fulfill.

How many people even get a chance to think about doing something like that?

It wouldn't be like I was starting out as a 90-shooter. I could get down to where my handicap is two or one or even zero if all I did was practice. I have my driving range and putting green right here and I can play any course I want.

Let's say I sink $30,000 or $40,000 into trying to make the tour qualifying school or play the mini-tour or something.

Why not do that? I daydream and I ask myself: "Why not, Rich? This is a dream you've always had and never got a chance to nurture. The journey would be the reward."

I either had the economic struggles growing up and going to college or I was starting a career or I was running the Sports Arena. I've never had the backing. You look at the bios of the kids on the PGA Tour and most of them were country club brats. They've always had lessons and had their games critiqued. I'd bet fewer than .0025 per cent came from the caddying ranks.

I don't need backing now because I could back myself. I could take a year and give it a shot. It would be interesting from a personal standpoint. I may not make it, but I could say it was fun trying.

The pressure should not get to me. Not after what I have been through with Michael Jordan. I'm probably as tough mentally as anybody out there.

Chapter Six

The Celebrities

I had not had much exposure to celebrity and celebrities when Harry Cooper and I bought the San Diego Sports Arena in 1989.

This would change very quickly. My job was to fill the arena with celebrities, whether they be entertainers or athletes or whatever. I suppose wrestlers and circus acts could be classified as both entertainers or athletes...or maybe whatever.

Regardless of whom my guests might be, part of my job was to make them and those around them comfortable so they would opt to return. These were guests I had to strive to keep within their comfort zones, unlike golfers such as M.J. If Rod Stewart, for example, wanted M & Ms, just the yellow ones, he got yellow M & Ms.

In both 1991 and 1992, we had one of the most active venues in the country.

We were fortunate at the Sports Arena to have hosted the likes of Bruce Springsteen, Frank Sinatra, Dolly Parton, Gloria Estefan, Cher, Neil Diamond, Randy Travis, Michael Bolton, U2, Billy Idol and Pavarotti. The list of personalities stretches onward to include talents such as Hulk Hogan, Terry Norris and, of course, Michael Jordan.

At first, I was co-owner. This suggested an aloof state in

which I let the hired help do the day-to-day chores. This wasn't going to last, because I wanted to take a hands-on approach to the facility. Desirous of playing an active role in the arena, I chose to engage on a day-to-day basis as director of operations. This put me in the interesting position of being above the president as co-owner and below the president as director of operations.

Nobody else really wanted to deal with the many problems in operations. Labor unions and logistics weren't really the fun stuff. We were trying to build a new arena and attract franchises and fill concert dates, but that was all the glamor stuff. Somebody had to get his hands dirty and fill the gap between the suits and the blue collars. The perception was that the prisoners were running the prison. I went downstairs with black pants, a white shirt and a tie and went to work.

The initial reaction was predictable. From the looks on the faces downstairs, I knew what they were thinking.

What the fuck was I doing down there?

However, I was welcomed with open arms on my first day when I rolled up my sleeves and helped install the new carpet in my office and rallied everyone to help with a new paint job throughout the guts of the arena.

They knew I wasn't coming at them with some ivory tower attitude.

I found it to be a good way to get to know the business. I didn't want to fake it. I was a young, energetic newcomer and I didn't want the rap that I didn't know the business. I went down into the bowels of the arena and made an office down there.

What I did was gain control of the building. I went through and negotiated four union contracts. I fired the labor contractor and fired other people who had been there for years but weren't producing. I gave the guys downstairs a real sense that upstairs cared. I brought order and a sense of pride to the event support people. They liked me and respected me for it. It worked both ways. I liked and respected them and appreciated what they were doing to make our facility the best it could be.

I drove my Jag to work and intentionally parked it downstairs outside my office for all to see. It was symbolic that the owner was there with them with his sleeves rolled up and working. The ushers responded to me and so did the changeover and engineering crews. We didn't have a first class building but we all worked together to create a first class operation. Every department made me proud.

———

One group I really wanted to get was The Grateful Dead. It wasn't that I was a big Dead follower, but they were good box office. I called my good friend Bill Walton, a San Diego guy and a bonkers Dead Head.

I had met Bill in 1989, not long after we bought the arena. Bill wanted to be very involved in the process of bringing an NBA franchise to his hometown. I had always admired him as a basketball player and I took a liking to him. He is one of those guys who is very easy-going, very easy to be around. For whatever reason, he liked me too, even if he wasn't a golfer.

Bill, in fact, introduced me to Larry Bird, who had been his teammate late in his career with the Boston Celtics. Talk about a down-home guy. We sat around at the Rio Hotel in Las Vegas during his "NBA Hoops Golf Classic" in 1990 and shot the shit, Walton, Bird, myself and Oklahoma coach Billy Tubbs. They drank beer and I stuck with my favorite libation...cranberry juice.

I didn't get to know Bird very well, obviously, in the two hours we were together, but he let his guard down a little bit because of Walton. I could relate to Bird because he's a country boy, a country hick out of French Lick, Indiana, instead of Raysal, West Virginia.

Bird was telling us how either his boyhood home, or maybe it was a friend's home, had an outhouse, but he didn't always use it. He said most of the rooms had dirt floors. He was laughing about how funny it was that he could just about take a piss anywhere.

You know what he did then? He excused himself and went to the bathroom, presumably indoors.

What I really wanted was for Walton to introduce me to The Grateful Dead. They were his buddies and I needed a go-between because the Dead had had a very bad experience with the San Diego police early in the 1980s. There wasn't any romance about it, because I wasn't a true fan. I wanted the Dead strictly as a business proposition. Three days with the Dead could net the building a quarter-million dollars.

Bill loved the Dead. We made a pact. We'd bring the Dead to San Diego.

We went to our first Dead show, my first anyway, at Shoreline in Mt. View, California. I had had been in Phoenix attending my golfing buddy Eric Weinberg's bachelor party and playing golf with Freddy Sarno. Brother Rob was there as well so we flew to San Francisco, where Bill and Kerry met us at the airport. We jumped into a limo and headed for the Dead show.

"Come on, Rich," Walton said, "let's go backstage and I'll introduce you to the guys."

I was reluctant at first. I don't like to force myself into people's faces. I don't like to intrude on their space. I was hoping for a casual rather than a formal introduction.

The first guy we met was the late Bill Graham, the famous rock promoter who later died in a helicopter accident.

"Bill," Walton said, "I want you to meet Rich Esquinas. He's the owner of the San Diego Sports Arena."

I got my first taste of Bill Graham's legendary temper. He went into a rampage and tore me another asshole about the San Diego arena and all the problems down here. He went on and on and on.

Walton was trying to interrupt him to no avail.

Graham finally exhausted himself and came up for air, presumably to fuel another explosion.

"Bill," I said quickly, "I'm a new owner. I'm here as an ambassador to tell you we want The Grateful Dead. Our venue is different now, I'm a hands-on guy and I want The Grateful Dead...and other bands you control too."

That chilled him a little bit. Walton and I still laugh about how Bill Graham turned me over his knee and spanked me about having a rough city and a bad venue.

After our conversation, Bill and I strolled onto stage right and listened to the Dead jam. It was fun looking out at that sea of Dead Heads. Kerry and my brother were both jealous when they saw us up on the fringe of the stage from their seats in the 15th row. Afterward, we stayed at the Dead's hotel and all got a chance to mingle.

I ended up going to three Dead concerts and we finally got their ears. We got everybody down to our Arena Club for a decision-making meeting. We had the people representing the Dead, their production guys and all their wheels. We had everyone from our end who might be remotely involved, including representation by the San Diego police. I was still fearful, because everything had to go just right.

It got down to one big question. The Dead's Denny Rifkin addressed a San Diego police lieutenant. I don't know exactly what Rifkin's role is with the Dead, because that group doesn't really have an organizational chart, but he was a heavyweight at this meeting.

"How will you treat us?" Rifkin asked.

"We'll treat the Dead like we treat any other rock band or show," the lieutenant said with seeming assurance.

I thought it was a good response and the lieutenant thought he had said the right thing. He was saying that he did not perceive the Dead as a problem. He was saying not to worry.

I thought, "Right on. We're in."

What he said turned out to be "dead" wrong. The Dead wanted to be treated favorably, not like everyone else.

Here I had painstakingly sat through three Dead shows, which was tough for me. That wasn't my crowd. I was totally out of my element with the hippies and the tie dyes and everyone on some kind of trip on whatever makes them fly. Plus, my GQ-style of dress made me stand out more than Walton, standing there seven-feet tall with his shaggy red hair.

I was backstage every show, chatting people up and pumping them on coming to my arena. Everyone was cued up for our meeting and the lieutenant says what seems to be the right thing and the Dead takes it wrong.

Walton and I felt very empty. We never did get The Grateful Dead to San Diego. And we never got the NBA either.

———

Having lived in a hamlet in West Virginia, a black neighborhood in Columbus and the melting pot of New York City, I became almost a multi-cultural, multi-lingual person. It served me well in San Diego when I started operating the Sports Arena.

I'm not saying I am fluent in English and French and German and Italian, not by any stretch of the imagination. The only foreign tongue I can even touch is Spanish and I could hardly deliver a State of the Union address in that language.

What I am saying is that I speak a lot of languages, a lot of tongues, within the English language.

In my work, that has been my greatest trump card.

I can talk shit with the brothers, the black artists and their people, and I can talk haughty with the people on the opera board. I can speak both urban and urbane. I can assimilate with the black community or La Jolla socialites. I can speak high finance and marketing one minute and get down to labor negotiations the next.

On one occasion, when I had Pavarotti's people in my office,

U2's people were waiting outside. I had "New Age" waiting and the highest sense of music culture you can have right there in my office. I loved both cultures with equal passion.

———

What struck me most about the artists coming into the arena was how different they were. We had the prima donnas, all pretentious with their Tinseltown illusions and their dispro-portionate perceptions of their own values. And we had the normal people who just happened to be famous.

Thumbs up to Frank Sinatra, Dolly Parton, Billy Joel, Kenny Rogers, Randy Travis and Cher.

Thumbs down to Axel Rose, Public Enemy and Andrew Dice Clay.

One of the first concerts we did, or at least had scheduled, was Rod Stewart. He cancelled not once, but twice, when we already had people in the building. He was about to appear in Los Angeles and he wanted to give his voice a rest because he thought it was raspy, which seemed to me to be its normal state. He rescheduled a couple of weeks later, and staged a splendid concert, but those cancellations were embarrassing as we were getting underway in our newly-acquired venue.

We had situations with Public Enemy and Guns 'n' Roses which were much more ticklish. In fact, things we got into with those people were downright scary.

Axel Rose, the lead singer with Guns 'n' Roses, was in the locker room for the first of two nights we had them scheduled. This was nice, except he was trashing the locker room and saying he wasn't going to come out and play. He was saying he was going to quit the band.

I was dealing with his personal manager and the promoter and they were telling me Rose was taking medicine because he was prone to drastic mood swings.

We had a hard time getting him out and he finally came out and said he was only going to play four songs. This would have been almost like playing nothing at all. That was how the 14,000 crazy people in the arena would have reacted. They had already waited two hours and they were already in a surly mood. This crazy man playing only four songs would not have been much of an improvement on disappearing out the back door.

Rose may have been depressed, but my stress level was soaring off the scale. It would have been a helluva lot like a 20-foot putt for $50,000, except I had some control over a 20-foot putt. I didn't have any control over what this guy might do.

My operations guy and I were on the radio with the security guys and the police department, trying to prepare for what might happen if Rose bailed after four songs. We would have to find some way to manage what would be a very unhappy crowd. We were prepared to hit the lights and deal with it.

Meanwhile, we were watching and listening as Rose went on stage. I was gambling (and hoping) that he would get to that fifth song and keep on going. I breathed a hurricane-magnitude sigh of relief when he hit that fifth song and kept on singing. In fact, he put on a helluva show. Maybe his rush was in getting everyone else on edge.

My momma never told me there would be nights like that.

The standoff with Public Enemy was different. It started with a backstage fight between our in-house security and the band's security. That was nasty enough, but the situation had the potential to get a whole lot more dangerous.

Public Enemy, at the time, was easily the hottest rap group around. Their new album just went platinum inside one month, a first for a rap album. They were what you called social rappers as opposed to melodic rappers because much of their music is about the plight of the black man. In truth, they were hard core social rappers representing hard core black Americans.

Since it was not unusual for Public Enemy concerts to take on a violent edge, I had 200 security guards and 25 gang-detail undercover cops in the building. There were 30 uniformed cops in and around the building.

Understand now that Public Enemy travels with Black Muslims. These were the guys, more than 20 of them serving as private security, who got into the conflict with my in-house security. My security ran a few of them out of the building.

Flavor Fav and Chuckie Dee, the lead singers with Public Enemy, were incensed. They declared that they were not going on stage until the Muslims were allowed back into the building.

Now I was in a real bind. I was always a big believer in backing my own people. I had stressed this in building the rapport I had developed with my people in all aspects of the operation. I had stroked them to underscore the confidence I had in their judgment. My people had acted with confidence knowing I supported their judgment.

If I let the Muslims back in, I would have a problem with my people. I would be undermining the rapport I had so painstakingly developed.

I called a summit conference in my downstairs office. I had Flavor Fav and Chuckie Dee and the rock promoters. I had Phil Quinn, my general manager, who was scared shitless. I had three Black Muslims and the band's tour manager. I had my security people and the police department. There were 16 people crammed in there.

I thought to myself: "If these people don't go on stage, I have a problem with the crowd. If these people do go on stage, I have a problem with my people."

No question, I had a problem, period. Nobody wanted to act on it. One of the promoters wanted to cancel the show. Chuckie Dee said he wasn't going on.

As I was entering the office, one of my stagehands pulled me off to the side and said: "You need any help, we're all here backing you."

He told me some of the guys had guns in their cars. I chilled that idea. We didn't need a gunfight at OK corral in the bowels of the Sports Arena with nearly 10,000 antsy people anticipating a concert. We didn't need Eliot Ness taking on Public Enemy. It was bad enough having my grandfather—remember Sheriff Chafin—getting gunned down by a fugitive in a whorehouse.

There were a lot of racial overtones in that little office and a lot of guys were yelling and screaming. It got down to nigger this and nigger that. I had to make a decision.

"OK," I said. "I'm going to let everyone back in but the two guys who started the shit. They stay out. And I don't want the other guys on the stage or around the stage."

Everyone agreed. Public Enemy got its guys back and my guys maintained control. I don't think anyone was 100 per cent happy, but the arrangement worked.

I was to experience tremendous stress playing golf with Michael Jordan, but I never had to worry about my building being torn apart.

———

Nicer things happened in my office, like the night I walked in and Billy Joel was sitting at my desk having a snack. I was dressed nice for the show, and he laughed and kidded me.

"Hey man," he said, "you don't have to dress up for me."

"Billy," I grinned, "this is for your fans."

I felt flattered. He was teasing on the square. For whatever reason, I've come to put a premium on nice clothes. I know clothes don't make the man, but they can be a measure of self-pride. OK, go ahead and call it ego.

I always dressed in black pants, white shirts and stylish silk ties for our events at the Sports Arena. I felt the co-owner should present himself nicely. I even wore ties when my sleeves were rolled up and I was doing dirty work backstage.

Ties are sort of my trademark. I usually wear white shirts, silk ties, because I get all the color I need out of my ties. I have

*Tallying up
our score
---and our bets---
was never an
easy chore.*

*Ali had me in stitches
when he got on my case
for bringing him all the
way from Chicago and
presenting him with a
poster commemorating
the 20th Anniversary of
the Ali vs. Norton fight.*

*Chatting here with
Charles Barkley and
Bill Walton.*

Julius Erving may have been the star on the basketball court, but my wife Kerry is the star of this picture.

My regular group: Me, Sarno, Weinberg and Heitzinger.

Harry Cooper, my partner in the arena, and Dolly Parton were a couple of Southerners who hit it off.

David Robinson had a few inches on me, but I drove a golf ball a lot further. He played behind my group twice when the Dream Team was in San Diego.

Maybe I could make a career out of color commentary. Promoter Dan Goossen was helping me out here on a cable show.

Tammy Wynette, Harry Cooper, Randy Travis and myself. I broke out my string tie for country artists.

*The Great One played
in an exhibition game
in the arena.*

*One of our early rounds.
Smokey Gaines (left)
introduced me to M.J.,
Michael, club hostess,
Adolph Shiver--M.J.'s
yakking buddy--and me.*

*Herb Williams and I
share Ohio State
University as our
alma mater. He
played in several of
our All-Star games.*

We had a big match with these guys, University of San Diego basketball coach Hank Egan (left) and former San Diego State basketball coach Jim Brandenburg (next to me). We bet $2 with the coaches and a lot more with each other.

Kerry gets a hug from Clipper owner Donald Sterling at a black tie fund-raiser.

I went toe-to-toe with Don King over an Orlin Norris-Bobby Czyz title fight recently. It didn't work out for either one of us.

Myself, a friend of M.J.'s,
Leon Parma and Michael.
Leon is a friend and one
of San Diego's shakers
and movers.

To
Richard
E, Hulk Hogan

Two hulks ...OK, only one
Hulk. Wrestling was always
one of my favorite events.

James Worthy and I
go casual poolside at
La Costa.

My biggest gamble at the arena was by far and away my commitment to boxing.

Orlin Norris, one of our frequent fighters at the arena, is the #1 ranked Cruiserweight in the world.

Oscar de la Hoya was one of our headliners on an ABC Sports telecast early in 1993.

Archie Moore hasn't missed a single one of our boxing cards. I wish we had had them a few years earlier, when he was such a great champion.

Terry Norris has defended his world title twice at the arena.

Here we are on the first tee at The Farms, probably deciding whether we are going to take mulligans.

Cliff Levingston, me and Spud Webb at a party before one of our All-Star games in the arena. Cliff's daughter is the one slightly smaller than Spud.

On my right, long time friend, Chris Vittorio, on my left, Bob Arum of Top Rank. My first beard ever...and last.

colors a rainbow could not imagine exist and I have designs that would blind Picasso.

Of course, when someone like Randy Travis came in, I wore a string tie. I wore my Armani tuxedo for Pavarotti. I like my artists to feel at home.

Jordan, Adolph and The Freds got a kick out of my clothes. They nicknamed me GQ.

———

I've always been sensitive to black artists, and I've always enjoyed them. I like black music, not so much rap but hip-hop. And I found the black artists to be very accessible.

Some of my feelings probably went back to growing up in a neighborhood that turned black. I could talk the language. We became known as the arena where certain black artists were treated well, which was not the case everywhere they played.

I went to the Soul Train Awards up in Los Angeles in the summer of 1990. These are the big musical awards for the black community and I thought it was important to be there. I took Leslie O'Neal, the Charger football star, and we rode to L.A. in a limo, watched the awards and mixed it up with Bobby Brown, Young M.C., Heavy D and the Boys and a lot of other black entertainers.

Over the years, we had all the top black entertainers in the arena. We had M.C. Hammer, C and C Music Factory, Kid 'n' Play, Bel Biv Devoe, Queen Latifa, Boys to Men, LL Kool Jay, Young M.C., Janet Jackson. No, never Michael Jackson, but I'm not sure he knows whether or not he's black anyway.

Hammer played our venue three times, once when Michael Jordan was in town staying at my house. I was a little nervous because Hammer was coming to San Diego from Las Vegas and I had heard from one of his handlers that he was having a bit of luck on the tables.

"I heard they had a helluva time getting Hammer out of

Vegas," I told M.J. "I've heard he's made $100,000 playing craps."

Hammer did make it to San Diego, and I tried to get Michael to go down to the arena with me for the concert. He just didn't want to get involved in the hassle, even sitting backstage. I asked one of Hammer's people to invite him up to the house to meet Jordan and he couldn't or wouldn't make it.

I don't know for sure, but this may have been a case of two egos expecting the other to come to him. From M.J.'s standpoint, he might well have wanted to avoid the scene he thought might come with an appearance at the concert. He was so sensitive to that kind of thing.

On another occasion, LL Kool Jay asked me if maybe I wasn't a little young to be running a building. Kid wanted to know if he could use my plastic to buy some food.

Milli Vanilli went through the building in their heyday, which happened to be at a time when we had a chimpanzee as sort of a mascot. Either Milli or Vanilli, I'm not sure which one, was cracking on the other on how the chimp looked like him.

The blacks were like that. They were loose and accessible and fun.

Except maybe Public Enemy.

———

Boxing was by far and away the biggest gamble I ever took on a day-to-day basis running the Sports Arena. I was conservative in everything else, from union negotiations to bookings. Boxing was a long shot.

It's an old sport and it's a slimy sport, but I was trying to fill dates in the arena. As operator of the venue, I booked probably 20 professional fight cards over the last two years. I've pushed hard for it, but it's probably my riskiest venture.

Nobody else wanted to deal with it. I felt it was kind of like having a 32-page catalog with 31 pages of nice products. You have that last blank page and you may as well throw something in there.

The truth is that I've always been a fight fan and I saw opportunity here. We have a world champion living here, Terry Norris, and I thought his presence might create a demand for boxing that we could satisfy. We've had two of his fights and he comes to most of our other programs.

Terry's a great sports fan, period. I invited him to the locker rooms after one of our NBA games so he could meet M.J., given that he numbers among the millions who idolize Michael. We ran into Charles Barkley and my attempts at an introduction were cut short.

"Man, I know who this is," Barkley said. "This is Terry Norris, the world champ."

My interest in boxing actually dates back to my boyhood days in the Linden area of Columbus. One of my father figures was a grade school football coach named Lee Williams who taught boxing. He was a black man who was a leading advocate of boxing in Columbus. I've paid for almost every pay-per-view fight I could get my hands on, because I've always thought of it as a good sport that reflects the struggle of life type thing. I lived that struggle.

I got an opportunity here with a local promoter, Scott Woodworth. He would run the boxing operation and I would fund it and hope to capture an audience by marketing through our "pay per view" mailing list provided by our largest cable company. I thought it would give us a more rounded sports look, along with hockey and soccer.

I hedged my bet here, relying on experts in the industry for advice. I talked with Jerry Buss, and also Bob Arum, one of the big names in boxing promotion. It wasn't like I was doing anything on a whim.

Boxing has not exactly been a rousing success for the arena, what with $100,000 in losses in 1992, but I'm optimistic about it.

Harry and I have sold 50 per cent of our interest in the arena, but I have carved out and protected my investment in the boxing part of the venue. I'm willing to gamble on it.

I have been around all of the key players. I've negotiated with Bob Arum and Don King and I've dealt with all the networks. Home Box Office, USA, ESPN and ABC have all telecast cards from the Sports Arena. Just this March, I switched dates because USA wanted my card. When I get TV money plus the gate money, I can make a profit.

Weird things happen in boxing, but I like being around it.

Sooner or later, I'll get a break. Among boxing venues, the Sports Arena is already right up there. I'm a young buck coming up through the system and I'm still learning.

I know this gamble is going to pay off. Of course, that's what I always think when I am taking a risk. A gambler never thinks he is going to lose.

———

We have had very few people in the building I didn't like. We had difficult experiences with Axel Rose and Public Enemy, to be sure, but one artist, if you can call him that, stands alone.

Andrew Dice Clay.

He was rude. He was a jerk. He was difficult. I didn't like Dice Clay, at least off-stage.

There are usually layers of protocol to get to an artist, but I always made it a point to at least attempt to say hello and thank you for coming. I never forced getting my picture taken with a star and never asked for an autograph. I wasn't dazzled by these people. I was just cordially trying to resurrect the soul of the building and let our entertainers know they were appreciated.

I went up to Dice Clay's manager to say thank you and asked if I could have a minute with Dice Clay to thank him as well. He said Dice Clay was real nervous before he went on and suggested I come back after the show.

This was fine with me. I could understand nerves before a show. I had them on the first tee all the time.

I went back after the show, but Dice Clay was back in the locker room with a woman. He was back there doing his thing, whatever that might have been, and no one could go back there. I could have, as co-owner, but I didn't.

When he finally came out, he was real curt and rude like he didn't have time for anyone. He was sloppy and loud and real obnoxious. I swallowed my pride and tried to be courteous to wish him the best, but he kept on walking.

The inside rap on Dice Clay is that he's not good with industry people. Basically, I understand he craps on the people who helped make him. What he is, whatever that is.

━━━

Frank Sinatra and his people were great. I loved him. I introduced myself and he came on just like you'd see him in movies.

"Hey man," he said, "this is some joint you have here."

I was thinking, here was Frank Sinatra in a 27-year-old building fighting a bad rep and he was talking like it was some nice nightclub or maybe Caesar's Palace. It was so Vegasy the way he said it. I thought it was classic Sinatra.

We sent flowers to Dolly Parton, who was great. Harry seldom went backstage to meet an artist, but he wanted to meet Dolly. Being from Mississippi, he got along with her real well. Dolly's from Tennessee, but the South is the South and so are southern manners.

Kenny Rogers had played golf with Michael Jordan. I knew that, so I made the point of telling him we had that in common. We just exchanged pleasantries about a mutual friend. We didn't talk about what their stakes might have been, but there could have been major money on the line between the guy who sang The Gambler and M.J. You're talking two Dun and Bradstreets that probably look like corporate ledgers.

I could go on and on listing people who were nice and easy to deal with. Sting. Eric Clapton, ZZ Top, Randy Travis, Cher. They don't all come with warm and fuzzy anecdotes attached. They were just real people, good people.

———

Animals were frequent visitors to our venue, and I'm not talking about Axel Rose and Dice Clay. I'm talking things like circuses.

Ringling Brothers came through every summer for maybe a week. We've also had the Moscow Circus, which still stands second only to Pavarotti for highest one-day gross.

You would think something like a Ringling Brothers Circus would be a mammoth undertaking, a giant headache for a person such as myself. In truth, it's an old and seasoned organization. They know how to get in and out of buildings very efficiently.

The people themselves are unique. They are classic carney people, a little bit scrungy and worn but seasoned. They know what to do because they do it over and over again in towns throughout the world. We're just another stop on their interminable road.

The animals are no problem either. They are as seasoned as the people and the people know how to handle them. We don't have to worry about lions roaming free backstage. We don't have to feed the elephants peanut M and Ms or anything. There's no fuss at all.

The circus people come and set up their little village in the parking lot and go about their business. The tough acts are the ones who haven't been around the block, who need to have their hands held.

One of my favorite acts is the World Wrestling Federation. Vince McMahon, the owner, has to be one of the more brilliant marketers in the country. He does a great job of blending the electronic media with live events and he has gone beyond that and into the marketplace with toys and video games.

If I remember correctly, six of the top 10 pay-per-view events have been WWF's Wrestlemania. Their shows have beaten the likes of Hagler vs. Leonard boxing and a lot of other things that would be surprising.

Not too many arena presidents would admit they are actually WWF fans, but I will. It's all just so farcical. It's as if they are putting everyone on and they know it. They almost become caricatures of themselves.

The fans are loyal and high energy. They might be religious and faithful and believing or they might be like myself, simply entertained by the entire scene. I laugh and have fun as much at what's going on outside the ring as in it.

As is my modus operandi, I always went backstage to see these characters. Hulk Hogan has played our venue a number of times, including shortly after a controversy broke out about his supposed use of steroids. I was afraid he would cancel but he was there. He brushed the whole controversy aside and said the media was blowing it out of proportion.

One of the most enjoyable things about such a venue was that every act, regardless of its nature, seemed to bring a life of its own. The building would always be the same, but the atmosphere would be different.

I might go to work one day and deal with petite skaters such as Peggy Fleming, Jill Trenary and Katarina Witt and go to work the next day and deal with apes such as WWF's Hillbilly Jim, who must have been from West Virginia.

It made for an interesting venue...and it made for an interesting job, especially for a workaholic.

Chapter Seven

The Rivals

I had two reasons for going to the 1990 NBA All-Star Game. First and professionally foremost, Harry Cooper and I were like ambassadors for San Diego in its efforts to get a franchise and this was a good place to shake hands. Second and personally foremost, Michael Jordan would be there and this would be a good time to renew our rivalry.

At about 1 o'clock in the morning the night before the game, after a long evening of glad-handing, I was just settling down when the telephone rang.

It was not an intrusion. It was M.J.

"What's going on, E-Man?" he said.

"It's going good," I said. "How you been doing? You've been looking pretty good."

"Wanna play tomorrow?" he said.

Michael never was much for small talk and perfunctory accolades. He gets to the point. There was no question what he wanted to play. I knew it wasn't H-O-R-S-E, that basketball game kids play in the driveway.

"Absolutely," I said.

"We'll go out to my buddy Ray's house," he said.

Another homeboy, I thought.

"Fine," I said. "What time?"

"Meet in the lobby at 7," he said.

Getting up in time for my TM and yoga, that would give me maybe five hours of sleep. That would be enough. I had my priorities.

M.J. was waiting with a rented white BMW. I tossed my clubs into the trunk and away we went. Here it was NBA All-Star weekend and we talked about virtually nothing but golf all the way to the course. It never occurred to me to ask about his buddy Ray, and he never volunteered.

We walked up to the driving range and there was his buddy Ray.

Raymond Floyd.

I was going to play with perhaps the greatest basketball player of all time as well as one of the greatest golfers of all time. I had played with touring pros before, such as Gary Hallberg in one of the Shearson Lehman Open Pro-Ams here in San Diego. I had also played with Scott Simpson, a San Diego guy who had won a U.S. Open. But now I was going to be playing with the winner of the 1969 and 1982 PGA Championships, 1976 Masters and 1986 U.S. Open. Looking back now, I note that Raymond never won as much in a year as I was to win from Michael in one week a year later.

"Hey, M.J.," I said, "I didn't know we were playing with Raymond Floyd."

Jordan just shrugged. This was his good-side style, tossing in little surprises like they were nothing. He liked the fact that he had caught me off guard. And this wasn't gamesmanship. This was just being nice. M.J. is hands down the king at this sort of thing.

Raymond is a Miami guy, but he went to North Carolina. I wondered if he and Jordan were friends because of golf or their alma mater. Probably both.

Anyway, here we were on Raymond's track. He is the host PGA professional at Turnberry Isle Yacht and Country Club, a very exclusive course in No. Miami Beach. I half expected to run across Ted Kennedy or Don Johnson. Ray did point out Julio Iglesia's home across one of the fairways.

One thing that is common knowledge about Ray Floyd, other than him being a great golfer, is that he is one of the best players on the tour with his own money. Other guys, you understand, can play for purse money, sponsor's money, on the tour, but they're not that good under pressure when their own money's on the line. Raymond could play for his money or Buick's money. It made no difference to him. That elevated him one more notch in my eyes.

We moved toward the first tee and there was Speaker of the House Tip O'Neill. He was not part of our group, but we all exchanged niceties.

I was ready for the ritualistic dance of numbers on the first tee.

"Raymond," I said, "I'd be disappointed and all my friends would be disappointed if they knew we played and I didn't have a nice wager with you."

See, even us swaggering, machismo gamblers can present a polite, respectful side when the situation merits it. I had had the little nervous rush you always get when you unexpectedly run into a celebrity, but I had quickly adapted. And there's always a rush of excitement during the ritual on the first tee.

"What are you?" he asked.

This is not golfese for checking ancestry, but rather asking about your handicap. I told him I was a six, which told him I usually shot in the mid to high 70s.

"I'll give you 10 shots," he said.

We played for $100 five ways. It wasn't a very vigorous negotiating session. There was not any grinding on the tee. He was probably easy on me.

M.J. and I played for the same wager, which was conservative by our standards even then. Neither one of us had been playing as much as we would like to play. I was tied up with the Sports Arena and he was tied up with the NBA season. We played even, as always.

I'm not going to say I didn't have nerves twitching and tingling all over my body. The bigger and better the opponent, the bigger the rush. Opponents don't come any better than Raymond Floyd.

I got off the tee like I had been hitting 1,000 balls a day off my back deck. I hit tremendous drives for the first five or six holes, well beyond both Raymond and M.J. When my drive is on, it's the strongest part of my game. It was on.

"Michael," Raymond said, "have you set me up with a hustler?"

It certainly was flattering to hear such a remark from Raymond Floyd, but I didn't exactly hustle him out of his life savings. In fact, he shot a rather tidy 68 and I shot a 78. He took me one way for $100.

M.J. and I played even and not a penny was exchanged. I don't know what he did with Raymond, probably the same as I did.

After we played, Raymond was kind enough to have us over to his place for lunch. With Mrs. Floyd and the children fussing over M.J. and taking pictures, I just couldn't resist.

"Mrs. Floyd, I'm a big M.J. fan but your husband is one of my all-time favorites. Could you take a photo with him and I."

"Sure," she said. "Let's go in his den where all his trophies are".

We had a little photo session in his den, which was filled with trophies and magazine covers. I really felt a sense of history and tradition standing with Raymond Floyd next to U.S. Open and Masters championship trophies. There was one picture of Raymond with President Bush, whom Michael probably didn't recognize.

Raymond's home was a beautiful ranch home with an adjoining waterway. I make mention of the house because of a terrible thing that happened the only time I have seen Raymond since that day. He was with Bill Comrie, a wealthy Canadian whose brother Fred had bought the San Diego Gulls hockey team from Harry and me. Raymond and Bill came to a Gulls game at our arena just before the Torrey Pines tournament in 1992. Ray's house burned down that night and he obviously had to rush back to Florida. I couldn't help but think about all those trophies and magazine covers, as well as all the other beautiful things in that house. M.J. told me later the trophies had been replaced.

When we finished lunch at Floyd's house, we were short of time to get back for the All-Star Game. No problem with M.J. He cranked the BMW up to 80 and 90 miles per hour and tore for the hotel to get his gear. I swear, if the Indianapolis 500 was run between a golf course and an arena, Michael Jordan would leave Michael Andretti in his dust.

We pulled up to the hotel and the lobby was a mob scene, likely because it was not much of a secret where the players were staying.

"E-Man," Jordan said, "you've gotta run some interference for me."

I swung his golf bag kind of sideways in front of me and plowed into the lobby. We went through a wave of people to get to the elevator. I don't know if I felt more like a bowling ball or a pulling guard, but I cleared a path.

Michael Jordan was late to the arena, at least in relation to when the players were supposed to arrive, but he was there for the game.

Personally, I had enjoyed one of my most memorable days of my life.

———

One of my chores, in terms of golfing with M.J., was to try to keep things simple.

It wasn't easy.

Everyone wanted a piece of him.

We had greenskeepers coming up and asking for signatures

on flags. You'd be surprised how many times there were five or 10 basketballs in the pro shop after our round. Golfers would just happen to hit stray shots onto our fairway hoping for a chance to say hello.

A hilarious thing happened to us once when we were playing Bear Creek with Freddy Sarno. At least I thought it was hilarious, because it struck at M.J.'s ego.

We had just finished nine holes and we wheeled our cart into the snack shack to grab a soft drink and, in M.J.'s case, the inevitable candy bar. I looked down the sidewalk and saw a maintenance vehicle barreling our way.

"Oh, oh, Michael," Freddy said, "I think we have a live one."

M.J. grimaced. The cart screeched to a halt and the guy jumped out and hurried up to Michael, with a scorecard and pencil in hand.

"Mr. Cooper," he said, "could I please have your autograph."

M.J. really grimaced. We were all laughing so hard and fighting so hard to keep it inside. This guy thought he was asking Michael Cooper for an autograph. I don't know what M.J. signed on that scorecard. He acted like nothing had happened.

Another guy popped up with a pair of BVDs he wanted M.J. to sign. Maybe that guy thought Jordan was Jim Palmer.

In most cases, Jordan was pretty good at avoiding distractions on the course. He would see people coming and be on the move. M.J. has a good technique for keeping moving and avoiding eye contact. He's become a pro at dodging those situations. He wanted to focus on golf, period. Even when we would come up on the group ahead of us on the tee, where he would be a sitting duck, we'd pull up 30 or 40 yards away and busy ourselves with our scorecard, which usually took a bit of figuring.

Getting onto the courses was not usually a problem, unless it was like a Saturday morning or we were trying to play on short notice.

My calling card had significant clout because of the tickets I was able to wheel and deal as president of the Sports Arena, plus whatever prestige went with the title. I could give you a recitation of which pros liked which events, which ones were hockey freaks, which ones went to all the WWF shows, which ones preferred rap (not many) and which preferred rock. Unless it was really an unusual circumstance, it would just be enough to say I was bringing VIP guests.

If I got into a bind, I'd say: "Look guys, here's my problem. I've got Michael Jordan. Can you help me?"

Once in awhile, they'd apologize and say it was just too crowded or maybe they had a tournament. That was fine. We didn't want to put anybody out, and avoiding an over-crowded course was just fine with M.J. We got so we finally stopped playing Stardust, because it was always such a zoo. We stayed with more private places off the beaten track.

I was making things as easy as possible for Michael. He's liking my stuff. I managed the golf course part. He didn't have to worry about it. I'm setting him up with good games on good courses with good golfers. Not only am I not one of those who's always asking for signatures, I would frequently tell playing partners not to bother him with that autograph crap.

Even something as routine as having dinner, as in going out to dinner, was difficult to do with Michael Jordan. He can't do anything without being pestered. It's as though fans think he is public property.

I wanted to set up dinner for Michael and his wife Juanita at Mr. A's, one of the better restaurants in San Diego. You don't get the rank-and-file in there. The steep prices take care of that.

The owner's son, a friend of mine who runs the place, made arrangements for me. He set up a nice little private room and popped the cork on an expensive bottle of champagne I had ordered. The Jordans, appreciative and gracious, had both their privacy and a very good dinner.

When you're dealing with Michael Jordan, you have to take care of little things like that. I call them maintenance issues.

My guys, my regular group, were really enjoying this opportunity to play golf with one of the legends of sports.

Ron Heitzinger noticed the difference both in the clubhouse and at work.

"All of the sudden," he told me, "we were hooked up with Michael Jordan and we were looked at in a whole different light. After our first few matches, an old man sat down next to me in the clubhouse and introduced himself and asked me what M.J. had said to us on the third hole."

I couldn't remember anything in particular about the third hole that would have prompted such a question. Maybe the old man was cruising by on an adjacent fairway and happened to look over and see M.J.'s lips moving in Ron's direction. More than likely, he was gawking at our group. OK, maybe not our whole group.

The thing about M.J. was that he blended so well with us when it came to the golf itself. We all played even and M.J. was right there with us so we didn't have to go through all the grinding on the first tee over who was getting strokes from whom.

M.J. was also getting comfortable on a social and conversational level.

"He was kinda quiet that first time out," said Eric Weinberg, who's kinda the quiet guy in our group. "He didn't know Rich that well and he certainly didn't know us. We had a whole different feel for him after we started playing. He'd get into the jiving and yackety-yak and he was fun to be around. He even got so he knew our names."

Heitzinger, through his role as a substance abuse expert, had done a lot of work with athletes, collegians mainly but pros as well, and now here he was playing golf with the world's greatest athlete.

"As soon as Michael saw we weren't going to put him on a

pedestal," Ron recalled, "we could jaw with him and talk shit with him and tease him both on the golf course and in a social setting. We weren't just filling tee times. We'd play cards..."

I once hosted a card game at my house. It was probably Ron's personal favorite moment, more than any 35-foot putt for a birdie or a great shot out of the sand to save a par. Ron had a big night. He said later he made more money playing cards that night than all of the golf added up. Michael was there with Adolph and one of the Freds.

We were playing guts. It took guts because anyone who stayed and lost had to match the pot and the money would sit there until the next hand. The guy who won took what was there. When the pot got up there, you could be craving a win but scared to death you'd lose.

The pots probably were not tremendously stimulating to Michael. He could toss $250 the way most guys tossed quarters.

When the pots started to grow, M.J. would sense the other players were getting out of their comfort zones. He would dare them to stay with him. He would go without as much as peeking at his cards. This was more of that gambler's machismo. You had to have a strong hand (and a strong heart) to stay, because there was no telling what he was holding. He didn't know and he didn't care. He could afford to try to buy the pot because it didn't make any difference to him if he lost it.

With $550 in the pot, Ron looked at his hand and he had an ace of spades. You only got three cards and M.J. needed to pair up to beat it. M.J. wasn't looking yet.

"You aren't going to look?" Ron said.

Michael shrugged and Ron stayed. Ron confessed to me later that he had accidentally gotten a glimpse of M.J.'s hand and he knew it contained no pair.

Michael rolled a queen high.

"One of us," Ron said, "is going to put $550 back in the pot."

Shit-talking Ron was enjoying this moment, knowing goddamn well he was going to win. He turned the first two cards, a 6 and a 10, licked the back of the third card and slapped that ace of spades onto his bald forehead. He looked M.J. in the eye, raked in the pot and then watched as Jordan put up $550 for the next hand.

"I wish I could have had that on film," Ron said. "My uncle taught me that trick when I was 10 years old."

I don't know if Ron ever told that story at any of his substance abuse seminars. Probably not. It didn't make much sense, I suppose, to lecture on the evils of one abuse and use a gambling story to get an audience's attention.

However, Ron had come up with a way to get his audience's attention any way. All he had to do is talk about his association with Michael Jordan, about playing golf and socializing. He and Michael might not have exchanged Christmas cards or Valentines, but they were there together on a golf course and in my living room.

"It gave me a vehicle for talking with kids," he said. "I'd talk about playing golf with Jordan and anything I'd say after that would be like it came from God. I could get away from numbers, which tend to bore kids, and talk about someone they idolized."

And Ron Heitzinger himself was a little in awe of his good fortune, playing golf with Michael Jordan. Not only did he enjoy his own matches, but he knew there was something special about the games Michael and I were playing.

Quinn Buckner, a former star at Indiana and a former NBA player, was joking with him once.

"Ron," Buckner said, "would you be interested in writing a story about these matches for the National Enquirer?"

"Hell no," Heitzinger said. "I'd lose my seat."

———

I didn't learn much from an experience Michael and I had at Shadow Creek Country Club in Las Vegas in 1990. This is a very exclusive club at the Mirage Hotel. It is more of a toy for Mirage owner Steve Wynn than a private club with a membership, because there is no membership.

We were playing our golf when Buster Douglas and his entourage came tooling up in a golf cart. Wynn had just made something like a $30 million multi-fight commitment to Douglas, but he had to beat Evander Holyfield to get to the second and third fights. He had kayoed Mike Tyson and he had big money on the horizon.

And here he was cruising around in a golf cart when I thought maybe he was supposed to be doing his road work. You know, running to get into condition.

At the time, I didn't think much about it. After all, I was playing golf with the world's greatest athlete and meeting the world heavyweight champion, another hometown Columbus guy at that. That's pretty interesting company.

When it came time for the fight, I went to Vegas with Bill Walton. We were ringside when Buster got busted by Holyfield. We liked Buster so Bill and I were depressed, like we had lost The Grateful Dead.

Sitting in the lounge at the Mirage, we were commiserating when Johnny Johnson, Buster's manager and promoter, came up. He recognized Walton and introduced himself and I introduced myself and explained how he had represented my twin brother Rob when he was getting a tryout with the Cincinnati Bengal football team.

Johnson invited us to a party, but we thought it would be miserable in the Douglas camp. We politely declined. Then Johnson went on to tell us how he and his fighter had become alienated and how he had embarrassed Buster in front of his family because he hadn't been training properly. He said he tore into him and never had control of his fighter again.

Buster was out of shape. Buster wasn't ready. I had seen that on the golf course. It hadn't registered. I had bet $2,500 on Buster. Walton and I accepted an invitation to go to Holyfield's party, where we met Evander and had an upbeat evening with the new champ.

———

My games with Michael, from a rules standpoint, were pictures of decorum. They were absolutely honorable. Neither one of us would do the tiniest thing to try to get an unfair advantage. It did not make any difference whether our balls were lying in different zip codes, we both knew we could trust the other to play the ball in its original lie or call a penalty stroke to improve it.

In other words, no matter what the stakes, there was absolutely no cheating. Any matters of rules interpretation were always settled in gentlemanly fashion.

We both had our gamesmanship techniques, like me with the cart and him with Adolph, but we were always gentlemen and always stayed within the rules.

Weekend hackers would get a kick out of one luxury we allowed ourselves.

A mulligan. One. Michael always liked to hit a mulligan on the first tee. Sometimes we'd get to a course late and we wouldn't have time to warm up. Or we'd look out on the driving range and see a lot of people and figure it would turn into a zoo if M.J. went out there to hit balls.

Naturally, if Michael was going to hit a mulligan, I was going to hit one too. Sometimes we set up the games without mulligans, but whatever we decided applied to everybody.

Of course, there was even honor to the way we dealt with mulligans. You couldn't hit two balls and take your choice. No way. If you hit a second ball, that was the one you had to play. There was no going back and saying, "Aw, I think I'll just go ahead and play the first one." Once in awhile, a mulligan would get us in trouble that way. We got so we'd usually take a semi-respectable first shot even if we had a mulligan coming.

Gimme putts were something else. They were very, very rare when we played. We conceded very little and a conceded putt could be a missed opportunity to make a big swing in both the game and the stakes.

I was very strict in that regard and I think it bugged M.J. that I'd never give him, or anyone else, a putt. If I gave him a putt, it had to be real close. I don't mean inside the leather either. It almost had to be close enough that an earthquake would shake it into the hole. I used to enjoy being the last word and having everyone look to me to see whether a putt was good. I had just seen too many little ones missed under pressure. Before anyone hit on the ninth and 18th tees, I would make it a point to say: "Everybody holes out. No gimmes." It would introduce one more element of pressure.

The Banditos down at Stardust played inside the leather was good, meaning any putt between the blade and where the grip started was a gimme. Not in my group. Some of those 12 to 18-inch putts can be tricky when you're not used to having to hole them.

When guys would miss them, I never hesitated to rub it in a little bit.

"That's why I didn't give it to you," I'd say.

They would be fuming about that for the next few shots. More gamesmanship. It was more than just the putt. It was the residual psychological effect. And this was a golf game.

One thing M.J. and I made perfectly clear to the other guys in our group was that they should never fuck with our balls on the green. You know how generous guys can be when a ball comes up maybe a foot from the cup.

"That's good," they'd say, and start to knock the ball away, just trying to be nice.

"That ain't good," I'd say.

"That's good, Michael," they'd say.

"That ain't no fucking good," I'd say.

That would get him a little roused and he missed a few of

those in our 2,000 holes of golf. He'd give them to me once in awhile and I'd keep telling him I wasn't obligated to give them back.

"I can't believe you won't give me this putt," he would sometimes complain. "E-Man, you must be kidding."

"If it's so easy, M.J.," I'd say, "just knock the damned thing in."

With enough money on the line, maybe it wasn't so damned easy. Maybe it looked just a little bit longer and the hole a little bit smaller. That was me playing with him psychologically. That's gamesmanship within the rules. I wanted him to be forced to concentrate all the time.

It just got so I knew a putt wasn't good unless I heard it from him and he knew a putt wasn't good unless he heard it from me. We didn't hear from each other very often when it came to giving away free putts.

My therapist would have a fit, but I have to tell you my No. 1 piece of advice to people gambling on the golf course is never to give a putt. It makes for better competition...and better golfers.

In the four years that we carried our games, I can remember only one dispute. And that did not involve Michael and me.

It happened in North Carolina, on the 18th hole at Pinehurst No. 7. Adolph was about 150 yards from me when I was getting ready to shoot with a lot of money on the line. From that distance, he thought the ball changed position from one time he looked until the next. He was trying to call a penalty on me and he wasn't even in the game. He was just along yakking and being a nuisance.

Michael had no problem. He knew I would have called the penalty myself if I had illegally moved the ball. He never cheated and he knew I never cheated.

We kept an honorable game.

———

My rivalry/friendship with Freddy Sarno pre-dates the others in my group and he became a regular with M.J. and myself. He must have played 20 rounds with Michael and me. He's a little guy, sort of a bulldog. He's a gritty competitor who can be playing badly for nine holes and then pull it together.

His father having been a wheel in Las Vegas, Freddy was more exposed to celebrities than the others in our group. He was around household names since he was a kid playing at the Las Vegas Country Club. He played with guys like Jim Brown, Glen Campbell, Bob Newhart and Mac Davis when he was still in Las Vegas.

"This whole celebrity thing, in terms of being in awe playing with Michael Jordan, doesn't do much for me," Freddy told me once. "M.J. dwarfs the guys I'd been exposed to, in terms of magnitude, but it's still not that big a deal to me. I'm just more used to it because of the high stakes games and being around the type of culture I was exposed to as a kid."

Freddy likes the gambling side of golf, though. It has been years since he has played a round of golf without at least some kind of a wager.

"It wouldn't be the same," he said.

He has a theory about gambling among golfers. There are the guys out there for financial gain, in the gospel according to Sarno, and there are the guys out there for the excitement of having money on the table, taking risks with something to lose. He likes the excitement of the risk and parallels the chemical release to people who get their kicks riding roller coasters, except what happens on a golf course is so totally unpredictable. No one wants to ride a totally unpredictable roller coaster.

Freddy got peeved at Heitzinger once at Carlton Oaks out in Santee when Ron was beating M.J. and M.J. asked him for a press. Ron turned him down.

"You've gotta take a press," Freddy complained later. "Otherwise, you look like one of those guys out there for financial gain."

M.J. was peeved too. He called poor Ron a bald-headed mutha-fucker. So much for bashing Heitzinger. I too, after the round, tore into Ron for "lack of gaminess" and told him in the future to let me know if he was going to have problems. I would fill his seat with someone else. Ron never turned down a press again.

Like Ron, Freddy had these ideas about trying to bet into Jordan's wealth.

"To make it fair," Freddy explained once to Michael, "I should be playing you 10 cents on the dollar just to make it even. I should be playing my $100 against your $1,000 so our choke points are the same."

Now there was some Vegasy gaming wisdom!

M.J. had to drive guys like Fred a little crazy. He would be working his pencil at 100 miles per hour on our scorecard trying to keep up with where we stood, but he wouldn't even know where he stood with Fred or Ron or Eric.

———

The magnitude of the betting was always a mystery to outsiders. The magnitude of what Michael and I were betting was a mystery even within our group. Everyone had bets, and my guys revved up their normal levels when they played with Michael, but no one knew exactly what was at stake except for the two people involved.

All this secrecy, however, created myths and myths have a way of warping reality.

"You know what some guy asked me?" Heitzinger said one day. "He asked me if it was true that we were playing for 50 grand."

Heitzinger was dumbstruck. Later, as he recalled the summer of 1990, he said: "You know, if I lost maybe $100, and the story started getting around, by the end of the week the story's been told 10 times and I've lost $1,100. I just didn't want to talk about money. Some of the numbers I heard were unbelievable."

Unbeknownst to Ron, there were times when some of the numbers he heard were true. But they just applied to Michael and me.

People's perceptions hurt us one time. We really liked playing The Farms, an elite private club up in the elite Rancho Santa Fe area of San Diego County. They asked me if I was interested in becoming a member in 1989, not too long after they opened, and of course I was very interested. I sent in an application with a check.

Shortly after that, I took a Minnesota executive and dear friend named Mannie Jackson, Charger football star Leslie O'Neal, former San Diego State coach Smokey Gaines and Michael out for a round of golf. Jackson, an executive vice president with Honeywell, was working with us, trying to bring black ownership to the NBA and a franchise to San Diego. All these guys but me were black, and I don't know to this day if that was one of the causes of what was to happen.

When I was at Michael's house in South Carolina later that summer, I got a rejection letter from the club. Kerry opened it at home in San Diego and called me with the depressing news. It was the first time I'd felt rejection at that level. I thought it was strange that they would reject me after wooing me so hard and closing on me.

One thing I heard was that it was a racial thing, that I had brought all these blacks out to the course. I felt a lot of anger when I heard this. I just didn't understand.

Or maybe they were afraid that next I would be showing up with unruly rock stars.

I also heard whispers that Smokey Gaines had said something to one of the cart guys about how much we were betting and it got back to the membership committee. I heard they thought we were gambling for way too much money and they didn't want that on their course. This was crazy. Smokey didn't know what in hell we were playing for and we were still at reasonable levels back then anyway. That's what perceptions can do.

M.J. ended up joining The Farms in 1990, so I tend to think we weren't dealing with racial stuff.

When a high-ranking committee member came back and asked me to let him know when I wanted to reapply, I never did. I'm not going to say I never will. But you remember back in high school when St. Francis invited me back after turning me away? I've had plenty of rejection and it will never sit well with me.

Some of these perceptions led to good-natured humor. Guys in the clubhouse were hearing rumors that we were playing for tremendous amounts of money, like tons of cash was changing hands out there.

Even Harry Cooper came up to me in the office and kiddingly said: "Hey, I hear you guys are betting Sports Arena stock against Nike stock."

I laughed. Before we were done, I guess they were all right about how much cash was at stake. It ended up being more than the most ridiculous rumors. But no one ever heard it from either of us...until now.

———

A dead giveaway to the potential magnitude of my bets with M.J. was our serious demeanor on the course. We weren't exactly like Lee Trevino or Chi Chi Rodriguez, cracking jokes and bantering and waving our putters like swords. We couldn't have been more straight-faced if we had been in church.

In fact, about the only place we would really converse was on the tee.

"You're pressed," I'd say.

"Coming back at you," he'd say.

Then before we went to our tee shots we would both

confirm the zeros lined up on our card just make certain we were eye-to-eye in agreement. And away we'd go.

Our behavior caused Heitzinger, for one, to be suspicious that we had stepped up to larger wagers.

"By that second year, 1990, I could tell that something was different," he told me. "You guys started keeping your own scorecard so we couldn't see how many presses and double presses and quadruple presses were going on. I could tell you guys were at a different level. You used to share scorecards with me, but I never saw those scorecards."

Ron might not have been able to decipher our scorecards even if he had been a cryptographer. Some of them would have been about as easy to read as the hieroglyphics on the wall of an ancient Egyptian tomb.

Our scorecards were brutal. Sometimes we'd need two of them, one to track the actual scores and the other to track the bets. One would be filled with single-digit numbers and the other would look like bond prices in the *Wall Street Journal*.

———

Poor Arsenio Hall was victimized *once again* in 1990. Michael was supposed to make an appearance, but we were on the golf course. This time he didn't call.

I didn't know he was scheduled to be on Arsenio's show until that night when Kerry and I were watching it. Arsenio was talking about what a good show he expected to have and then Michael didn't show. His producer told Arsenio, on the air for all of the viewers to behold, that M.J. was probably on a golf course somewhere in Southern California.

That was a good guess. My telephone rang and it was Heitzinger. He had been watching the same show. He had been flabbergasted that Jordan had passed up a chance to be on national television for a game of golf.

"Ron," I said, "Michael is on national television all the time."

Still, I thought Jordan was a little cold about it. That's a different side of him, a side I would see when trying to later negotiate his debt to me. I really don't think he could have flat-out forgotten.

———

Michael almost missed an obligation to play in Magic's mid-summer All-Star game in L.A. in 1990. We played 18 holes in the morning and then rode in caravan out to Carlton Oaks, which is 15 to 20 miles east of San Diego in Santee.

M.J. realized he was going to have to go like a bat out of hell to get to L.A. in time for the game so he asked if he could rent a BMW. This will probably get him another commercial. It had to be a BMW.

I called my wife Kerry and explained the situation. I'm not sure how excited she was about calling, but she did.

"I told the rental people I needed to have a BMW delivered to Carlton Oaks in an hour," Kerry recalled later. "They didn't seem too excited about it until I told them my husband was the owner of the Sports Arena and he was playing golf with Michael Jordan, and Michael Jordan needed the car."

Kerry rolled her eyes, as she often did when I was involved with M.J.

"Michael Jordan, Michael Jordan," she said. "Heaven and hell could have turned over and they would have gotten that car out there, if only they could get their pictures taken with him."

She wondered later if they even bothered to charge him for the rental. She probably had a right to wonder. On another occasion, she hired a Mercedes with a driver to take M.J. from our house in La Jolla to his hotel in La Costa. The $75 charge showed up on our statement.

I wondered later what time Michael got to the Magic game, though I read in the newspaper that he was late. He left Carlton Oaks at about 6:30 for an 8 o'clock game and the drive should have taken 2½ hours. M.J. had already proven to me he did not have to have a basketball in hand to execute a fast break.

———

Our betting was up in 1990, but it was not out of control like it would get a year later. By the end of the year, I owed him $17,000. As I explained, we weren't paying off on a round-by-round basis because it would have been senseless. Our check registers would have started to look like our scorecards.

I couldn't make it back to Carolina in 1990 to put a wrap on our "season," so that $17,000 tab was left dangling. It was a small amount so I told him on the phone that I'd pay him at the 1991 All-Star Game, since it was a pretty safe bet he would be there. Unfortunately, because of a concert or whatever, I couldn't get there. He wasn't distressed. He knew I was good for it and dropping $17,000 into his bank account was like dropping a bucket of water in the ocean.

The next time I saw him, before Game 4 of the 1991 NBA Finals in Los Angeles, I went up to his room and handed him a check.

I would hand him checks, very big ones, in 1991, but this would be the last one he would cash.

Chapter Eight

Mr. Corporate America

Michael Jordan may be the most recognized man on the planet. I swear there are people in Seoul, Sydney, Stockholm and Santiago who would recognize Jordan ahead of Bill Clinton or Boris Yeltsin. That may not be in sensible perspective, but that is what we have done with and to our athletic and entertainment heroes these days.

What these people earn is totally out of touch with reality, also beyond sensible perspective. All a baseball player has to do to make a million dollars a year is be able to hit .220. We were bidding to get Madonna to the Sports Arena and we were told we would have to come up with a $300,000 guarantee, which was out of the question.

Just today, I read in the paper that the San Diego Chargers will be paying an offensive tackle named Harry Swayne $2.7 million to play football this year. I would be willing to bet that the majority of people in San Diego have never heard of this guy and he is now the highest paid player on the team. I wonder what my buddy Leslie O'Neal, the best player on the team, thinks of this deal.

If there is a stairway to fiscal heaven, Jordan has to be at or near the top step. He might make $30 million a year or maybe $40 million. He may not even know for sure.

Counting M.J.'s money would be like trying to count the straws in a hay stack.

Is it possible to turn on either a radio or a television in America without hearing or seeing Michael pushing a product? Is it possible to walk through a mall without seeing a cardboard Jordan staring from a window?

Kerry was in the market the other day and there was M.J. on the shopping cart, hawking hot dogs. I turned on CNBC and they broke away from stocks and bonds to a report on M.J. opening a restaurant, as though this was so compelling it could not wait.

M.J. is a Chicago Bull player, but all of corporate America seems to be bullish on him. He is a Nike Bull, Chevrolet Bull, Wheaties Bull, Gatorade Bull and McDonalds Bull. You can ride him, wear him, eat him and drink him.

I can't tell you how many times people would show up at the golf course with Wheaties boxes for him to sign. I also can't tell you where in hell they found Wheaties boxes on golf courses.

Someone messed up when they named that North Carolina freeway in his honor. Madison Avenue should have been renamed.

I don't think Jordan or anyone else could have foreseen such a phenomenon taking place, especially if they had seen this gangly kid as a boy in Wilmington, N.C.

———

Michael was born in Brooklyn, but raised in Wilmington. North Carolina does not seem to have anything but medium-sized cities and this was one of them. It's the state's largest port, about 30 miles up the Cape Fear River from the ocean.

Michael never talked much about his childhood. He mentioned brothers once or twice, but he never got into his family and upbringing with any depth at all. It was almost as if he wanted to be more of a mythical character with no history other than what he is.

I know he wasn't anything like a sharecropper's son. His is not one of those tobacco road stories. He went to Laney High School in Wilmington and didn't even become a starter on the basketball team until he was a junior. He wanted to go to UCLA, which was better then, and he liked North Carolina State. He ended up at the University of North Carolina in Chapel Hill.

Michael's best years at North Carolina were 1983 and 1984, when he was The Sporting News college player of the year. Ironically, North Carolina won the national championship in 1982. It would become more than a coincidence that Michael's best years did not always coincide with his teams' best years.

Amazingly, he was only the third pick in the NBA draft. The Chicago Bulls really wanted a big center, but Houston grabbed Akeem Olajuwon with the first pick and Portland got Sam Bowie with the second. That left the Bulls with this kid who might be a big guard or might be a small forward or might not be much of anything at all.

No one could have known Michael Jordan would be everything.

The Bulls had been a bad team with an apathetic following before M.J. came along. They were suddenly exciting, though not as suddenly successful. What Michael couldn't do right away, or even very soon, was win them an NBA championship. He started winning scoring championships by his third year, but the Bulls did not win a title until his seventh year. That was 1990-91, when they beat the Los Angeles Lakers. They won again in 1991-92, when they beat the Portland Trail Blazers.

There had previously been considerable controversy about whether a team could win with such an individual talent as Jordan. Part of the controversy had to do with the Bulls' organizational chart, many suggesting Jordan was at the top, above the owner. He complained to me once, in a rare but insightful conversation about basketball, that the media had unfairly portrayed him as the perpetrator of the demise of former Bull coach Doug Collins.

All the Chicago players themselves had to be supporting actors to the star and Jordan was unmistakably the star. He was caught in a no-man's-land only he could inhabit, both blessed and cursed for his individual skills. Basketball, like maybe no other team sport, showcased individual skills, yet it did not always allow them to translate to team rewards.

Maybe Michael should stick with individual sports.

Like golf.

———

One of the reasons Jordan liked me, I think, was because his homeboys liked me. His No. 1 guy, Adolph Shiver, was around all the time. The Freds, Whitfield and Kearns, were around a little less, but they were definitely regulars in his posse. There were one or two others, including another Fred, but these were The Boys.

I could assimilate with his posse. I could jive with them and talk trash with them. I could listen to their music, though some of the social rap stuff didn't sit well in my eardrums. I have always been comfortable in a black environment, from the days in the black neighborhood in Columbus to my enjoyable dealings with black artists in the Sports Arena.

I have no idea what Adolph does for a living, but he is a guy who goes all the way back to Jordan's boyhood as a friend and teammate. I believe the Freds are college buddies from UNC, Whitfield an attorney and Kearns a mortician. They probably spend less time with Michael than Adolph does because they have real lives, which Adolph doesn't seem to have.

The Freds were nice guys. It wasn't like they had attached themselves to Michael as a way of establishing their own identities. They would come along because they enjoyed the ride, but they didn't need the horse. On a few occasions, they expressed their dislike for Adolph's exploits in this regard.

Adolph needed the horse. He rode M.J. through life. Even in the betting, when Adolph was chirping about side wagers, he was always riding his horse.

I tried to accept Adolph as a friend of Michael's who happened to be a character, but there were times when he got on my nerves and everyone else's. People tended to think of him as a pain in the ass because he is very verbal, very vocal, but I have always gotten along with him, maybe in spite of himself. He calls me GQ, because he likes the way I dress.

It seemed to me that Juanita, Michael's wife, tolerated Adolph, at best. Maybe that's a good word for the way most people deal with him. Juanita, though, happens to be married to the man Adolph serves as sort of a parasitical Siamese twin.

The flip side of the coin is that Adolph badmouths Juanita...in front of Michael.

I asked M.J. about it once and he said: "Adolph's Adolph."

That was a pretty good summary. His buddy's ragging on his wife, but that's just the way his buddy is. So much for taking it seriously.

In truth, I think Adolph has a little green streak. Juanita has come into Jordan's life and taken time that used to be his.

"I've seen big changes in Michael being around Juanita," Adolph told me once.

He couldn't articulate exactly what those big changes were. That would have taken the conversation to a serious and analytical level, and Adolph never quite got to that level.

"Hell yes, you've seen changes," I told him. "The man's married now. He has a family. He's not back in the hood with the boys."

That was probably where Adolph wanted him...back in the hood with his homeboys.

———

Everyone wanted a piece of Michael. Everyone wanted to be close to him. Everyone wanted at least an autograph.

"Please, Michael," they'd say. "It will only take a second."

All those seconds and all those requests would add up to days and days of imposition. He was careful and cautious about picking the places he went and who accompanied him.

M.J. did a good job of insulating himself within the cocoon of his posse. In a sense, I guess, I was part of that posse for awhile.

Kerry was not a part of all that. In retrospect, I think I was insensitive to what she may have been thinking and feeling while M.J. and I were in the midst of our golfing escapades.

I know that now because I asked her about it...

> *I was always excited for Rich, but I always resented the hell out of his relationship with Jordan.*
>
> *How would you like it if this guy Michael Jordan would call, like crooking his finger, and your husband dropped everything and took off for six and seven days at a time without wondering what you're going to be doing for those six or seven days?*
>
> *I specifically remember one year we were supposed to go to the Night in Monte Carlo gala, a benefit we both really enjoy. Rich was off with Jordan and didn't even think about it. He didn't realize he had missed it until he was looking at a picture and I was there with my cousin.*
>
> *Whenever Michael called, Richard was there. It was like he had Michael Mania. Everybody seems to have it.*
>
> *I saw a different side of Michael one night he stayed here at the house. Adolph, one of the Freds and Juanita were here too.*
>
> *Rich called me and told me they're going to play golf, but they're going to drop Juanita off. He*

tells me I should take her shopping. I felt shy and maybe a little resentful, but I did like shopping and Juanita did too!

With Rich, Michael is Adversary No. 1. M.J. is much more of an adversary because of who he is. Rich is playing golf, the whole thing, with the No. 1 person in America. You ask nine out of 10 people who they'd like to do something with, and they'd probably say Michael Jordan. Isn't that shocking? I've never been able to figure that out, but I'm not a sports freak either.

This was one of the nights M.C. Hammer was appearing at the Sports Arena. Richard was always excited about Hammer coming to town, but Rich didn't see Hammer that night. He didn't go because Jordan was in town.

I went through four years of my husband working 16 and 18 hour days, not being home, not having time to do things with Felicity and me because work came first. M.J. calls and he can just disappear? I was not a happy camper.

Now all of the sudden I was supposed to go along with The Michael Game and Michael and Juanita were coming to stay at the house, maybe with some guys with them. I called Adelaide's that day and had $500 worth of flowers delivered. I even purchased new linen for their bed. Let's see Rich complain about those bills. Michael was coming.

How did it go? They dropped Juanita off, she was pregnant then, and I took her shopping. She's a lovely person and it was obvious he adored her. My friend Kimberly was there for the weekend too and went with us. She hit it off with Juanita. We shopped all day and got home just a few minutes before the guys got there.

Michael came in and said: "I'm starving. Isn't there anything ready for dinner yet?"

This really put me on edge. Should I order out, or cook? After all, I was presenting dinner to Michael Jordan! I had asked Juanita what he might like for dinner and she told me he loved pasta. Fine, I prepared a nice eggplant parmesan with pasta and a Caesar's salad.

While Jordan was in the kitchen teasing me because dinner wasn't ready, Juanita disappeared down the hall into the bedroom. She didn't come out until late in the evening. After all, she must have been tired. She was pregnant and we had been shopping all day. She never ate a thing.

Later, Michael came back into the kitchen, looked at what I was preparing and sort of wrinkled his nose.

"What is this?" he asked.

"Parmesan and pasta," I said, actually thinking I would get a smile of approval.

"I'm a seafood man," he said. "I only like seafood."

"But Juanita said you liked pasta."

"That's only during the season."

This is when I learned that pasta actually had a season, and tonight it was out. Things were not going well and I wanted so much for them to go well and make it a great experience for Rich.

The guys decided to play cards. Ron Heitzinger was there too. That was the night he beat Jordan out of a pot with that card on his forehead.

First, though, we had to come up with an acceptable surface for playing cards. I never realized there were unacceptable surfaces for cards. For tennis maybe, but cards? They were going to play on a glass top table, but Jordan said you couldn't play cards on a glass top table.

Fine. I had a beautiful table cloth from Spain. It had geraniums on it and it was one of my favorites. I'd hate to say what I spent on it.

"We can't play on that," Jordan said. "You have to have a white table cloth to play cards."

Fortunately, Kim was keeping people distracted fixing drinks. She was making something with papaya, pineapple, orange juice and vodka. She's darling, probably around 5-feet tall and extremely shapely. Fred and Adolph kept busy flirting with Kim, really flirting, while I was trying to find the right table cloth.

After the card game finally started, Michael called me over. He grabbed my hand. I was wearing a platinum ring with a two-carat heart diamond in the middle and two carats on each side.

"Show me that ring, Redhead," he said. "Richard E, you're gonna lose this ring tonight."

"Excuse me, Michael," I said, "but this is my ring and I'm not playing cards with you."

Michael kept going on and on about winning the ring. He was probably kidding but it got old.

"Michael," Richard finally said, "you've heard what the lady has to say about the ring."

Michael actually could be so fun. He fell out of his chair once, he was laughing so hard at the goings-on. He was like a kid, so worked up and so excited.

There was more than one side to Michael. He had been at the house many mornings waiting for

Rich for a golf game. I would fix him coffee and
toast and share the paper or watch CNN. He was
always polite and gentlemanly. He would always
ask about Felicity when he called.

Maybe that was why I was so caught off
guard by his requirements that evening. It really
wasn't like him. It might have had to do with
being around Adolph, whose mouth was running
the whole time. He seemed to change when the
homeboys were around, especially with Juanita
out of the room.

If that evening taught me anything, it was
that Michael Jordan is a human being like
everyone else. He has good sides and he has bad
sides, good days and bad days. He is not better
than anyone else and he's not worse.

I have to confess. I had never asked her what she thought
of all the golf I was playing and time I was spending with
Michael Jordan. Maybe I was afraid I would get the answer I
finally got, because Kerry is obviously not one to mince words.
She was also not one who would call a halt to the good time
she could see I was having.

In the end, I guess I was like everyone else when it came to
Michael Jordan.

I was blind.

———

Michael did not always get his own way. It just seemed
like it. I remember one time he wanted me in his foursome and
couldn't have me.

He was going to be in Las Vegas for the Evander
Holyfield-George Foreman fight and he wanted me to get
there for a golf game at Shadow Creek, Steve Wynn's Mirage
course.

I was in Los Angeles, so I detoured to Las Vegas. The Mirage was full so I checked into the Dunes. Our game was set for the next day, the day of the fight.

My telephone rang.

"E-Man," M.J. said, "you can't play. You're not staying at the hotel."

"You mean I can play if I get a room?"

"I guess," he said.

"M.J., I tried but they're sold out due to fight," I said.

"Let me get it," he offered.

I figured Michael had as much juice as anybody. He offered to bypass the front desk and go to the power guys. He said he would check.

No problem, I thought. I had Michael Jordan getting me a room in a jammed hotel the night before a major fight. The golf game would include Jordan as well as Steve Wynn and the legendary Julius Erving.

This was huge. What a golf story for my golf buddies. This would be power golf.

Michael called.

"Rich, I got you the rooms," he said. "Here's the name of the guy you need to talk to."

Then he called back.

"Rich, they don't want you to play," he said. "I don't know the story."

M.J. was very apologetic about bringing me into the town, but not into the game. He wanted to take me out to dinner afterwards.

"Michael," I said, "I understand and I appreciate your efforts, but I'm out of here. It's too crazy in this town just to sit around."

I took the next flight out of town. M.J. told me later he had had fun, but there hadn't been much gambling. That will take a whole lot of the fun out of a round of golf, regardless of the company...at least for M.J. and me.

I wasn't a Michael Jordan freaky-deak fan. I knew he was a great player, to be sure, and I always rooted for him to do well, but out of friendship rather than fanaticism. Our bond, or common ground, was gambling and golf. Kerry was right in that his status as perhaps the world's greatest athlete revved my juices, but I was far from starry-eyed at the mere notion of being in his company.

If anything, I think, the fact that I wasn't some kind over-zealous basketball nut made me a more appealing companion.

I was kind of M.J.'s way out of that whole basketball world. I wasn't a part of that world. I didn't want to be. I was a guy he could hang with, bet with, play golf with and kind of turn all the basketball off. We didn't sit around and talk hoops. We talked golf, our games, our shots, new clubs, that sort of thing.

M.J. has quite a network of non-basketball friends because he liked getting away from the basketball. It was almost as if he ran from always hanging with basketball guys.

About the only way you could set him off on basketball was to say something about Detroit, especially something nice about Detroit. He hated everybody on the Pistons. He talked one time about how he would beat Magic's ass in a one-on-one competition, but thought the whole idea was stupid. And he thought Larry Bird was a trash-talking hick.

When he was griping about perceptions that he ran the Chicago Bulls, I was amused.

Right, Michael. And the "G" next to your name on the roster really stands for guard rather than god.

Chapter Nine

Caper in Carolina

I walked into Michael Jordan's room on the eve of Game 4 of the Bulls-Lakers NBA Championship series in June of 1991 and it was standing-room-only. His father was there and so was his sister. Ahmad Rashad was there and so were the homeboys, a couple of Freds and Adolph. The Bulls were staying at the Ritz-Carlton in Marina del Rey, an oceanside bedroom community outside of Los Angeles. I checked in there too.

Under unfinished business from 1990 was the matter of delivering a $17,000 check for the losses I had incurred. My tab was clean. We were even.

I waited, of course, until we were alone to deliver the check. It was nobody else's business. Believe it or not, we actually had 45 quiet minutes when the others had wandered off.

Going one-on-one in that situation was unique, because it was in such command performance circumstances and he had so many friends and family around. In a more typical situation, during the season of almost interminable travel, Michael could be found alone in his room more often than not.

We talked a lot about business, money, the Sports Arena, his Nike deal. He didn't tell me about his whole financial picture, but it was kind of like money talking to money. He felt a level of confidence to share with me. He perceived me as a young, somewhat successful sports executive, albeit low-profile and unknown compared with him. Dan Quayle was unknown and low-profiled compared with Michael.

"What do you think of this pay-per-view idea, me going one-on-one with Magic?" he asked at one point.

I had heard a little bit about it but the NBA didn't seem very receptive, partially because of the precedent it would set and partially because the league didn't stand to get any bucks out of it.

M.J. didn't seem too excited either.

"I don't know why Magic would want to go through with it," he said. "He knows I'd beat him. My game's much more attuned to a one-on-one situation."

———

It wasn't often we talked basketball. Maybe this was a time we couldn't avoid it, being in the middle of the final series and all. Generally, I was his way out of that whole world. He could kind of turn that whole thing off when he was with me.

We talked some hoops and he told me the Bulls had the Lakers on the ropes, which they did. He talked about owning a European basketball team and I was thinking he could probably buy a European city, or country, instead.

The conversation wandered away from basketball to Nike and some of his other endorsement deals. I could rap money with him, though I was like most of the rest of the world in that my balance sheet looked like a midget next to his. Still, he respected my business acumen and opened up to me more than he might have with anyone but his closest advisers.

I asked him once about politics, but the subject didn't really seem to tweak his interest. That wasn't his world either, nor were racial issues. He told me he had been confronted by politicians and black leaders who wanted to use his influence to jump on certain causes, but he had steered clear.

"I just don't do it," he said, "because I can do better by not doing that sort of thing. I have more impact by not being that way. I can have more influence on society and do more good for more people by not taking radical political positions like Jesse Jackson and others sometimes took."

I guess this was his way of saying he would lead quietly by being a wholesome example.

He would be Michael Jordan, star athlete and star person, and that would be enough.

Our relationship worked because he could see I wasn't dazzled by the star athlete part of the picture. I wasn't one of those groupie types who would kiss his ass because of what he could do with a basketball in his hands. I think he appreciated that. I didn't come after him for autographs, didn't ask to have our picture taken and didn't come after him for tickets.

In fact, I rarely went to games at all. I went up and saw him play a couple games in Los Angeles against the Clippers and I saw him play against Cleveland once in Chicago.

And he got me nice seats to Game 4 in Los Angeles.

———

The writers were making quite a bit of stir before Game 4 about a toe injury Michael had suffered in Game 3, but he wasn't sitting there packed in ice or wrapped in bandages or sounding all concerned. In fact, he never said word one about any aches or pains.

Michael had had a big game in Game 3. I had watched it on television, which was my usual vantage point if I wanted to see him play. I'd usually only watch the fourth quarter and see if it was heating up.

Game 3 really heated up. M.J. had to sink a basket near the end of regulation to send it into overtime and then scored six points in the overtime period. The Bulls took a 2-1 advantage in what was a best-of-seven series.

We did not look back on that game and we did not look ahead at Game 4. We were talking about getting together a golf match between Games 4 and 5. We had our priorities.

The Bulls won 97-82 in Game 4 and I went up to his room to say hello and congratulate him. He had 28 points and 13 assists. Everybody thought that injured toe might have given the Lakers a chance, but it must not have been as serious as everyone thought it was. That toe kicked the Lakers' ass all over the court.

I didn't notice him limping too much on the golf course the next day. We had a low-wagering game, maybe $100 five ways, and we ended up playing 27 holes. It was a strange number, but we were prone to tacking on an extra nine holes here and there. We couldn't play any more because he had to get to a team meeting.

I think I beat him one way, which was more than the Lakers could say.

———

Michael and Co. wrapped it up in Game 5, but I couldn't be there. I had business in San Diego regarding the sale of a percentage of the Sports Arena. The buyers asked for another one of many extensions they requested, causing a surge in work load, so it was too late to get to the game. It would have been great partying with M.J. after the championship game, a once-in-a-lifetime experience, but I could not sacrifice my duties at the arena.

I was getting much busier on day-to-day operation of the arena, since I was assuming the responsibility of the presidency. I was a very hands-on president, so I needed to spend a lot of time downstairs behind the scenes as well as in the executive offices upstairs.

During this time, I was very involved with trying to make boxing successful in our arena. I was working with Terry Norris, a local San Diego hero and a champion. I scheduled an August bout with a challenger named Brett Lally. This kept me both busy and interested.

It had to be August of 1991 before Michael and I got together for another summer of adventure.

M.J. was in Southern California for Magic's all-star game and some Nike shoots. I know about the Nike shoots because they rented our Sports Arena basketball floor for 10 grand and put it down in a studio.

I went up to L.A. to meet him and we played places like Hillcrest, Brentwood and Bel Air. We certainly did not have to settle for muni tracks. We went first class.

Checking my date book, I see directions to Hillcrest on August 3. We played there in the morning. I finished weak, hit a ball into the woods on 18 and made a 6. He had a 5 and ended up beating me out of about $10,000.

Obviously, we're betting more heavily now. I came out of a few days in L.A. down probably in the range of $15,000.

Magic's game was, I think, August 4 and our San Diego game was August 6. We came down to San Diego and played Fairbanks Ranch and Rancho Santa Fe. I was starting to come around now and beat him, our tab going back and forth, staying in the $5,000 to $10,000 to $15,000 range.

On the day of our All-Star game, we played 18 holes at a Four Seasons Resort course up by La Costa called Aviara and 18 holes at Rancho Santa Fe Country Club. The guys at Aviara there were easy to get along with. The pro, Bob Christy, and the director of golf, Jim Bennington, understood the problems bringing Michael out. One Monday, when they were closed, they opened the course just for us.

We played one of those nondescript games where not much happened with money changing hands and then headed for the Sports Arena for our All-Star game. We went into my office upstairs rather than the locker room and Michael used my shower. He was sitting around in his underwear in my office just relaxing and eating some pizza I had brought up.

Michael remembered he was supposed to meet a writer from Sport Magazine in the locker room, so my director of operations and right-hand man, Mark Neiber, escorted him up to the office. The guy wrote in the article about being summoned upstairs, I guess sort of for an audience with the lord of basketball. He didn't know who I was. He thought I was a public relations guy, maybe M.J.'s personal goffer.

Michael had been after me to join him and Charles Barkley and Adolph on his private jet the morning after the game and fly back to Chicago. I was really torn. He wanted to hang out in Chicago and play golf for a couple of days and I really wanted to go. He had leased this jet, a comfortable plane which seated maybe 10. It sounded like fun, sitting there playing cards and being waited on by the stewardess.

I just couldn't do it. I was underwriting this Norris fight and Norris had a promotional luncheon the next day. I just couldn't leave, not responsibly anyway. I had to take care of business in the arena.

Jordan's golf clubs were in my trunk so I had a friend, Chris Butler, run them down to Brown Field, where M.J. was waiting with his plane. He might leave his luggage behind, but not his golf clubs.

——————

I caught up with M.J. on August 8, when I flew into Chicago. He had his limo driver waiting for me at the airport. I should have been wearing track shoes. We raced to Michael's house, threw all of our gear into a minivan and then raced to the M.J.'s jet. We headed for Charlotte, N.C., playing cards all the way.

The next few days reminded me of that movie Cannonball Run, where all these people are going coast-to-coast at break-neck speeds. The difference was that we were going from Chapel Hill to Raleigh to Durham to heaven knows where. I felt like I was living on fast forward.

*Mike Horton, a semi-regular at our outings,
gets a handshake from M.J. while I look on.*

*Myself, Adolph and M.J. at my home playing
cards. Shit-talking Ron Heitzinger is at left,
probably raking in a pot.*

Magic played his first professional game in our arena against the then San Diego Clippers. I played a few hands of cards with him when he was here with the Dream Team.

I treasure this picture of myself with Raymond Floyd and a few of his many championship trophies.

Ray Floyd

2/22/90

Dear Rich,

I am enclosing the pictures we took at my house the day we played golf with Michael.

As you can see, my wife is not going to win any awards for photography!

Best regards,

Raymond

RF:mcn
Enclosures

I had a chance to visit with the legendary Elgin Baylor when I attended a brunch for the Los Angeles Clippers before training camp one year.

Donnie Simpson of television's Video Soul with me at M.J.'s United Negro College Fund benefit tournament.

Harry, Charles Grantham and myself. Charles is executive director of the NBA Players Association

Frank Sinatra's line about what a nice joint we had was one of my favorites. He's pictured here with Harry Cooper, Kerry, Harry's sweetheart Valerie Preiss and myself.

Our arena would have wrestlers one night and people like Jill Trenary the next.

Visiting with young M.C. during his "Bust-a-Move" days.

I have played in Spain, Mexico and Portugal, but this game was on China's only golf course.

A couple of hillbillies from West Virginia. The one on the right is a little better known.

Ali was nice enough to come to one of our pre-fight parties.

A frequent foursome: Eric Weinberg, myself, M.J. and Fred Sarno on the first tee at Jack Nicklaus' Bear Creek Country Club.

Dave Winfield has worn a few uniforms in his great career. This was a different look.

Wayne Gretzky, King owner Bruce McNall, Harry Cooper and myself appeared at a press conference to promote a Kings exhibition game.

Our final round in 1992. Note the circled area which shows the $1.252 owed me minus $250K minus $50K and minus another $50K which left a balance of $902K. This was negotiated down to $300K to settle what had been nearly an 18-month ordeal.

We made a 140-mile trip from Raleigh to Charlotte in two hours, hitting 90, 100 and maybe even 120 at times. Michael has a partnership in a Nissan dealership and he had borrowed a Datsun 300ZX Bi-Turbo. We had the top off and we were both wearing these expensive designer shades. In fact, M.J. had on the ones he wore when he hosted Saturday Night Live. We were on top of the world. He was feeling great because he was the world champ, at least the Bulls were, and I was feeling great because I was up on him about $20,000 in our games at the time.

Later in the summer, they were naming a freeway after him. I don't know if this was the freeway, but M.J. was driving like he owned the road.

We're buzzing down the road with Adolph and the boys behind us. Michael's a good driver at high speeds because he has many fast cars and he's used to driving them fast. We weren't being reckless, just being fast, whatever that means in terms of being reckless.

If the police stopped us, we figured we'd just talk our way out of it.

"Just talk nice to the policeman," Adolph had bellowed out as we pulled away.

We never got stopped. We went on through driving hard and fast, very hard and very fast. You gamble hard and fast, then you drive hard and fast. The gambler's psyche doesn't change.

———

The whole reason for this whirlwind drive to Charlotte was that Adolph was having a party and Adolph had told all of North Carolina and half of Georgia that Michael Jordan was going to be there. I can't speak for M.J., but it appeared to me that Adolph was his best buddy, his No. 1 hanger-on. Michael may stiff Arsenio Hall and George Bush, but he wasn't going to leave Adolph twisting in the breeze. He had to be there to salvage his buddy's credibility, even though he did grumble a little.

Besides, Adolph could put together a good party. He threw a birthday party for Michael at the 1991 All-Star game, which happened to be in Charlotte. One of the rap groups we'd had at the arena, Kid 'n' Play, had entertained. Being around M.J. gave Adolph a little bit of pull in circles he couldn't have imagined in their playground days.

We got to Charlotte and settled into Adolph's condo for a couple of hours waiting to go to the party. It was a small but nice condo, modestly furnished when you could see the furniture under the clothes strewn all over. I recognized some of Michael's ties and clothes lying around the condo. He must pass them down to his friend when he tires of them. Michael has so much money he can probably just toss things rather than bother sending them to the cleaners.

The party was at a hotel. Adolph's condo couldn't possibly have held the crowd. There had to be 300 or 400 people. I sat at the center table with M.J. This had to be about as relaxed as I had seen Michael in a social setting, even though it was a mob-scene in terms of numbers. These were his people, a lot of old college friends. He could loosen up in North Carolina far more easily than he could in Chicago or San Diego.

This was one of those rare times when we were stuck in one place and vulnerable to the approaches of strangers. That caused this to be one of those rare times we were vulnerable to approaches from strange women, or at least women we didn't know. I'd hate to call them strange, because they weren't bad, if you know what I mean.

We had a couple of girls hitting strong on us. I'm probably not a bad looking guy, but I'll have to swallow my ego and admit some of the attention I was getting had to do with my golfing buddy. I felt a need to escape so I headed for the suite we had taken at the hotel. M.J. was not too far behind me.

We had to tee off at 8 o'clock the next morning so we had to leave the hotel at 6:30. Once again, we had our priorities.

———

San Diego is known as America's Finest City.

At least that's what it calls itself. One of the reasons is the weather. It's always nice. San Diego's TV weathermen could probably tape their forecasts in January and take the rest of the year off. They ought to be ashamed to cash their checks most of the year.

I make this point to underscore the fact that M.J. and I were blessed with one bright and sunny day after another on the golf course.

One exception was a day during our Carolina caper on the Governors Cup Course in Chapel Hill. Naturally, this was a 36-hole day. The weather was threatening and threatening some more and finally, with about three holes to play, we were hit by a good steady rain.

"What do you think?" Michael asked. "You wanna keep playing, E-Man?"

"I'm from Ohio," I said. "I'm used to this stuff."

I took the opportunity to thrust a needle.

"M.J.," I said, "you're not thinking of quitting, are you?"

We had a newspaper reporter with us for the day, I think from a Greensboro paper, but we still had some nice bets going. He was asking what we were playing for, but we were just laughing it off as modest stuff, more for the fun of it.

In reality, though, we had some bucks on the line and we were neck and neck. I was starting to get some momentum and I definitely did not want to quit.

We kept going and I made some money. Football players may be able to play in the mud, but Michael must have been out of his comfort zone.

We probably did more socializing on this trip than during any other period of our relationship. It probably had to do with M.J. being on his own turf with all his buddies. It wasn't like trying to go out to a club in Chicago or a pizza parlor in San Diego.

"Let's go out and see some of the town," Jordan said one evening. "Let's mix it up a little bit."

Town? We had been moving so quickly I wasn't even sure what town we'd be seeing.

"Sounds good to me," I said. "Let's go."

It did sound good, getting out, but he had caught me off guard. We were sharing a suite and the usual drill was that his buddies would be over for cards. It was always golf all day and cards all night. The gambling season began when the basketball season ended.

Now he wanted to go out in public, of all places. I figured it to be a small place owned by a North Carolina alumnus. I assumed it had a quiet back room away from the madding and maddening crowds.

I was wrong. M.J. was going public. He was world champ and he was feeling good about it. I think he wanted to get out where he could taste it, savor it.

Adolph called ahead to this club and told them we would be coming. I didn't know anything about the place, but it was an all-black nightclub in a huge warehouse.

When we pulled up in front, I knew there was no way this wasn't going to turn into a scene. I had some expertise in "crowd management" and this was going to be a problem. The place was packed, but we moved through and leaned up against the bar before anyone realized what was going on. It was dark enough that you weren't going to pick up faces and recognize people very quickly.

I stood out in the crowd, however. I was white. My therapist would have pointed out where once again I didn't fit.

Once everyone realized Michael Jordan was there, we had to scramble because people started swarming.

"Come on, GQ," Adolph said. "Let's throw down some interference. Gotta get settled in here."

Adolph and I and a couple of bouncers got us all moved to the disk jockey's stand, where the bouncers roped off a section for us. M.J. had to be treated in a special way even when he was trying to get out among 'em.

It was one of those disco dance places and we had our own dance floor in our roped-off section. There was dancing and carrying on and a lot of girls hanging around giving us some play.

"Who are you?" one girl asked me. "You his agent?"

It was more like she was asking me what the hell I was doing there. I swear I was the only white in the place.

"Naw," I said. "Just a friend."

I was getting special attention because I was with Michael and attracting curiosity because I was white. This was a classic black bar, a place where everyone went. I wondered, though, what it might have been like if I hadn't walked in with Michael Jordan. I wondered if I was being accepted only because of my companion.

After awhile, it got to be kind of crazy with autographs and pictures and women hanging around, but we stayed and closed the place.

About those women? We were never casual about that sort of thing. We went back to our suite as we always did...with nobody.

———

Losing at golf or losing at cards bothered me, as competitive as I am, but it did not bother me as much as losing a $2,500 Cartier watch.

This bugged the hell out of me. My compulsive TM was to blame. Sort of. We had checked into a hotel suite after another 36 holes of golf and the party was starting. The cards were on the table and the posse was ready for an evening of staying in rather than going out.

I was tired. We had played the 36 holes and I had been doing TM for 19 years twice daily and my biorhythms were getting out of synch. TM was and is something I'm gladly addicted to and I have to have it.

But where? I just couldn't ask everyone to leave for maybe 30 minutes. M.J. knew about my TM, but I didn't care to share it with the others. Most people think it's weird or freaky.

I excused myself. I said something about going someplace quiet to call Kerry at home. Instead, I went out to the car. It was the quietest place I could find unless I went and sat on some log, which, in retrospect, wouldn't have been a bad idea.

I took off my watch and set it down on the console. I went off into my own world. Relaxed, refreshed, I went back to the suite 40 minutes later.

And I forgot my watch. When I noticed, I didn't worry about it because I thought it was in my golf bag. I didn't realize it wasn't until I got back to San Diego and unpacked.

I learned later that the car dealer, M.J.'s partner, had found the watch. It must have ended up under the seat or somewhere. The dealer turned the watch over to Adolph, of all people. As far as I know, he still has it. I've asked for it, but I haven't seen it since.

It shows how much I'm into TM.

All of this wheeling across the landscape and dealing on the golf course brought me near the end of my visit. We were at Pinehurst, which, to golfers, may be as close to heaven as you can get.

The tab was running, of course, and the first 18 holes at Pinehurst pushed it to $25,000 in my favor. This was about as high as it had gotten. It was about to get shoved out of control and, ultimately, out of sight.

With 18 holes remaining to be played, Michael asked for a one-down press game and doubled the units. The one-down press game meant you could press, essentially add another bet, any time you lost a hole. These presses can add up very rapidly. We were now playing for $2,000, plus a premium of $10,000 on a medal bet. And, we frequently exercised options to put additional presses upon demand. God, we would put one or two presses frequently on one hole making for a sequence of one and zero with major consequences on *every* hole.

Michael wanted a chance to get his money back. In gambling terminology, this is called chasing. He was risking more money to retrieve what he had lost. He more than did that.

This second 18 we played that day was a big one for M.J. It would be an understatement to say that he came back significantly in that round. The one-down press bets caused a whole sequence of action to pile up over the round.

By the time we were done, Michael was up $48,000. For those who don't have an abacus handy, let me do the math. He had accomplished a swing of $73,000 over 18 holes. Our reasonable betting had flown out the window.

After the round I felt flustered. Shortly after walking off 18, I uncontrollably blurted: "Give me the same chance I just gave you. Give me a chance to get even."

This is where you get into the gambler's psyche. It was getting dark and we had played 36 holes a day for a week and I wanted to keep going. I was down, but I wanted a chance to get even on nine more holes...and it was getting dark. It was absolutely crazy and it was all my idea. Now it was my turn to chase.

As always with us there was no resistance to stacking up the bets.

"Tee it up," M.J. said.

We were playing for $5,000 on one-down presses and

$10,000 on medal play and another $10,000 on match play. I was going after a $48,000 deficit on nine holes in the gathering darkness and I faced the possibility of losing double that.

I think both of us were a little nervous, probably me more than Michael. After all, he was playing with my money.

I had side bets with Adolph, and I was starting to learn that Adolph was a distraction and a tool for Jordan. He was becoming a disturbance. I started to see the strategy. Adolph was getting real gamey about Jordan kicking my ass.

"GQ, you ain't gonna beat the world's greatest athlete," Adolph needled. "I've put all my money on my horse."

Adolph's shit could get old real fast. I kept putting extra presses on, above and beyond the one-down presses. I'd say to M.J. that I wanted another press and he would take it without hesitation.

We had our scorecard with the bets on it and the zeroes were piling up. We had holes with potential eight-press swings. Multiply eight presses times $5,000 a press and you get a feel for where the betting had gone. Those were very serious zeroes.

The last three holes were very, very serious holes. I kept tallying the numbers in my mind and I knew I could make a lot of money swing on those last three holes. It was a matter of turning presses where he had a one-hole advantage into zeroes and presses where we were even into plus-ones for me. There was potential for a tremendous swing, like playing the commodities market.

I lost the seventh hole and tied the eighth and we got to the ninth. If Michael got a par, I needed a birdie just to make the losses manageable. He still would have won $11,000 to $12,000, depending on where the zeroes fell from the presses. A mere par, no easy score in this circumstance, would put me down $98,000.

The ninth was a 235-yard par-three. We knew where the pin was because of playing earlier. However, because of the darkness, we couldn't see it. This was no way to play for the kind of money we had on the line, but it had been my idea to chase that debt in these ridiculous conditions.

M.J. hit a great shot, a three-iron directly at where we thought the hole should be. I hit a two-iron I thought might be *in the hole*. We didn't know for sure until we got to the green. M.J. was 25 to 30 feet short of the pin and I had a 20-footer from the back fringe.

The tension around the green was thick. We had built up a gallery of maybe 15 to 20 people. All Michael's homeboys were there and everyone knew what the numbers were because Adolph was spreading the word around. We never talked numbers, but remember that Adolph is a yakker.

I was sweaty and hot and worn out, this being our 45th hole of the day. My nerves were shot and my brain food was gone. I wished I could have slipped off into the woods and done 30 minutes of TM.

Michael was away so he hit first. I knew he would make his par. He left himself with a tap-in. It might have been a gimme in some groups, but not with me. Not with what was at stake. It was so close, though, that he tapped it in.

Now it was all on me. I had gotten myself into position. I could make a 20-footer. It was far from a gimme, of course. The green sloped down and away from me, which was hardly the optimum circumstance for a putt of such magnitude.

How important was this putt? If I make it, I'm down a manageable $6,000. If I miss it, I'm down $98,000 to Michael...and $20,000 to Adolph on side bets.

That was all, just a $112,000 swing on one 20-foot putt in the dark.

I backed off the putt a couple of times, trying to read a tricky green in the dark as well as gather myself emotionally. When I struck the ball, I thought it had a chance. The silence was unbelievable as the ball trickled down the hill toward the hole. I think the little group around that green sucked in all of the air in North Carolina. Even Adolph was quiet.

My putt slid four feet past the hole. My heart sank. It was the most frustrating and disappointing feeling I had ever had in my life. Here we had been going back and forth, tabbing $7,000 or $10,000 or $15,000, and now I was $98,000 down...plus the $20,000 to Adolph.

Suddenly, we were into huge amounts of money and I was starting to realize we were out of control. I was way past my tolerance level, which was basically around $20,000 to $25,000. I was sick. We were sick.

We walked slowly toward our cars. The whole group was quiet in an uneasy way. So much had been at stake. We packed our clubs into the trunk and M.J. settled behind the wheel.

"Michael," I sighed, "I need a week or two to fit all this together and I'll settle with you. I need to take time and catch my breath and work some things out."

I could pay, but not without considerable financial pain. I could pay, but I would have to figure out how to do it without Kerry finding out. I could pay, but I wasn't sure exactly how.

Michael was fine. He was a gentleman about it.

"No pressure, E-Man," M.J. said. "No problem with waiting 'til I get out to San Diego."

No pressure. No problem. I had all of two weeks to figure out what to do and how to do it. I thought about my real estate holdings taking the hit! Christ!

Adolph was a different story. He was pissed off. He wanted his money right then and there.

"You have to wait," I said, "but I'll honor the bet."

M.J. chilled Adolph, told him to settle down. I didn't need to be dealing with his shit. It was bad enough leaving town with a $118,000 debt hanging over my head.

I'll never forget how sick I felt. Remember that I was up $25,000 at one point earlier in this very same day. I was thinking back to putts I'd missed and shots I'd like to do over. With all those zeroes, any one shot could have made this loss reasonable rather than outrageous.

I rode with Michael to the hotel where the rest of the group was staying. One of the Freds drove me to Durham, where I had to catch a 6 a.m. flight to San Diego the next morning.

What made it worse was that business, a Bel Biv Devoe concert, was forcing me to leave. Michael had a match the next day with Dean Smith, his coach at North Carolina, and the legendary Jerry West. I would love to have played with them. And I would love to have had a chance to cut into that debt.

That's a gambler's mentality...chasing.

Chapter Ten

The Struggle

I knew now that we were out of control, totally out of control. I was down $98,000 to Jordan, plus $20,000 in side bets to that bastard Adolph. I was way beyond what I could sensibly lose.

Michael had beaten me on the square. We made the match and set the terms and I lost. It was simple as that, but oh how complicated in the aftermath.

I would find a way to handle that $98,000 Michael had fairly won.

However, that $20,000 I owed Adolph really griped me.

You see, if I had won that kind of money from Adolph, there was no way in the world he could have paid me. Michael always made it perfectly clear that Adolph's bets were his own. He wasn't going to pick up his buddy's freight.

Why bet with the guy? Adolph was always chirping on the side about this or that bet, doubling here, pressing there. He called it riding his horse. Jordan was his horse. I was always focused on what was happening between M.J. and me, so all of Adolph's stuff on the side was more of a distraction than a concern. I couldn't believe it when I realized what the number had gotten to with him.

As far as I know, Adolph hasn't worked a steady job since he got out of college. What I've understood from everyone around is that M.J. basically funds his life. Michael gives him money here and there and takes him on trips, even to road games during the season. They share a special relationship.

None of this translates to Adolph being good for $20,000 had I been the winner rather than M.J. It nagged at me that I felt I had to be good for it.

I had enough to worry about dealing with the $98,000 I dropped to Michael Jordan.

Kerry couldn't know. My gambling on golf, or anything else, had never been a subject of conversation at the dinner table. It was something I did that was my thing. This was part of my world she never cared to invade.

Once in awhile, we would talk in vague terms about how things were going on the golf course. If I told her I'd won, I would always decrease the number. I did this for a couple of reasons, one of them probably selfish. First, I didn't want her to know what we were betting. Second, I tell her I've won too much and she has things she wants to buy. I'd have to explain you live by the sword and you die by the sword. You win what seems a lot at one time, but you don't always win. You have to have that cushion for when you lose. You go in and buy something with my winnings and it takes away my gambling slush fund.

Kerry probably thought Michael and me were going back and forth like I always did with my regular group, though she undoubtedly assumed we were at a little higher level.

I was always keeping this fund at $25,000 to $30,000. That was my fun money, my go to hell money, my go to Vegas and blow $5,000 betting on the Super Bowl money. It went up or down according to whether I was winning or losing, but it always stayed in that range.

When I went to North Carolina and lost $98,000 to Jordan

and $20,000 to Adolph, my go to hell money was shot to hell. I had gone to North Carolina thinking I would be careful to maximize my losses at $25,000 if things went badly. This was the ceiling I had set when I was packing for the trip and thinking in a sensible manner.

When I told Michael I needed time because I didn't want Kerry to know how much money was involved, he told me he didn't mind telling Juanita about his gambling. That was fine until he owed me big bucks and he wanted time because he didn't want Juanita to know.

I was at the point where what I had lost could imperil my family's lifestyle. This is a dangerous point which strikes at the heart of the addicted gambler.

One of the phases a compulsive gambler goes through is the bail-out. You lose beyond what you can reasonably fund and start looking around for ways to cover your losses. You think of going to friends and family to borrow big money and maybe they will give it to you once without asking questions. That's already a problem, but it gets bigger if that money goes out the window too and you have to look elsewhere for more.

The next phase is desperation, which should not really need more precise definition or explanation. The compulsive gambler on a losing streak, in a losing mode, can become totally irrational in his approach to regaining his fiscal sanity.

I didn't know any of these terms when I was struggling with that $118,000 deficit. In retrospect, there is no question they applied to my frame of mind.

One thing I considered was refinancing the family home in La Jolla or the cabin in Ohio. I had more than $500,000 in equity on these properties. I had savings and I had cash too. I could get the money together, but the duress I was feeling was all-consuming. I was distracted and disturbed.

Every direction I looked, I could see Kerry. I definitely didn't want her to know. There were times when I thought I could sit down with her and figure things out, but I would always go back to trying to figure it out on my own. That's the gambler's mentality, staying in a self-imposed closet and internalizing irrational thoughts. It would be too logical to discuss a sensible solution with a loved one who would understand at least the problem if not the cause.

———

Kerry had been warned that I might have a gambling problem, but she hadn't really paid much attention at the time. It wasn't something she could comprehend. Not too many people understand that gambling can be an addiction, but Kerry couldn't even perceive of gambling on a most innocent level.

She first heard about Rich Esquinas and gambling when she made her first trip back to Ohio with me for my brother Rob's wedding. She had felt like she was riding with a knight on a white horse. I was her saint of a boyfriend.

Then my sister Cecilia and my mother took her out onto the porch and had a talk with her.

"One thing to watch for with Rich," they told her, "is that he had a gambling problem when he was in college. He had a problem gambling on college basketball and we're afraid his gambling might continue to be a problem."

I didn't know about this conversation until much later, long after I had gone into therapy and long after Jordan and I had gone off the edge.

The warning certainly had not deterred her from sustaining the relationship which has given us a beautiful daughter and a wonderful lifestyle.

However, I was curious about exactly what she was thinking at the time.

"I had this Southern Baptist upbringing," she said. "No one drank. Never. I never saw anyone drink. Here you were, and you didn't drink either. I certainly had never heard or seen anyone gamble. It was totally foreign to me."

They told her the story about my bookie Bo, though they didn't use his name. They told of how Bo hadn't paid me so Rob and I went over to his place to pay him a visit. They embellished it a little with a "hillbilly" spin unique to our family's ways of telling stories. They had us tearing his place apart and throwing his clothes out into the street. I'd like to have seen the look on her face when they were telling her this tale. Never mind, I don't think I would like to have seen that look.

Amazingly, Kerry never mentioned this little warning to me. She told me later she blew it off as an eccentricity of the past rather than anything to concern her in the present and future. She saw me as a down-to-earth workaholic who had outgrown such unimaginable conduct.

Her Rich could not be so stupid. Later, when what became my regular golf group got going, she knew we were betting on the games. This didn't bother her. She understood that these were just friends passing money back and forth, which was really what it was. She still couldn't figure out what motivated people to gamble, but this wasn't really gambling to her. It wasn't really gambling to me either, just a little incentive on the side to put some spice into our matches.

That may sound like a typical gambler's rationale, but it was true...at the time.

The gambling on the golf course was no problem, but gambling became a ticklish subject at the breakfast table when it once came home with me.

I don't remember the year, maybe as early as 1985 or 1986, but I was playing golf with a guy I'll call Joe who took some football bets on the side. I don't think you'd really call him a bookie in the classic sense, but he was booking bets.

We were both recognized as high stakes players in golf, meaning we'd go $100 when other guys were at $5 and $10, so we honed in on each other for a few matches. Gamblers do that sort of thing. They find adversaries at their levels almost instinctively, just as Michael and I had.

Joe knew I liked the Cincinnati Bengals so he started calling me and asking me about betting on some games. It seemed harmless enough to me. I didn't bet much with him, relatively speaking, and it was only a few key games over one season.

However, Kerry was not pleased with these Sunday morning calls to our breakfast table. She knew he was taking bets over the telephone and that made him bookmaker, a low-life bookmaker. To her thinking, the underworld was invading her kitchen. She couldn't believe a person she considered to be of such dubious character was calling her home. She didn't like him and she didn't think he could be trusted.

I liked Joe, though he was nobody I would chum with all the time. My bets with him never got out of control, except maybe on the golf course, but that was not the issue with Kerry.

Her inner sanctum had been violated. My football betting stopped and so did the calls. It was nothing I was compelled to do. I didn't get any rush out of taking the Bengals and giving Pittsburgh three points.

My football betting, before and since, has been limited to Super Bowl Sunday...and only legal betting at the casinos. I have hit seven of the last eight, usually for $5,000. I dropped my bet to $2,500 on the last one because of all the late hype on the Buffalo Bills. I'm glad I stayed with Dallas, but the damned Bills made me nervous.

The only places Kerry has ever seen me gamble are Las Vegas and Marbella, Spain. I guess that disturbed her too.

"Disturbed me?" she said, her voice rising in response to what I realized was an understatement. "It was like you were crazy. It was unbelievable to me. You'd sit at a blackjack table with like thousands of dollars in front of you and you'd put it all on one hand like it wasn't any big deal. I was so upset. To you, it's the game. It's not money. It's not winning or losing. It's the game."

No, Kerry, it's the rush of the game. As I sat in my own tumultuous world with my own tumultuous concerns, poor

Kerry did not know about the games I had been playing...and the games to come.

Kerry could not have known what my desperate mind was concocting as a solution for a problem she didn't realize I had. I would chase that $98,000 with another $98,000. And I would pay, if necessary, by refinancing my real estate holdings. I cannot even imagine how great the pain would have been had I blown that bundle, and I was really too irrational to think about it.

Had she known, she would have strapped me up in a straitjacket and frozen me under the ice in the Sports Arena.

Chapter Eleven

The Killing

I was about to make the biggest gamble of a lifetime I was living on the edge. I was $118,000 in debt after that fiasco in North Carolina. The only way to kill that debt, at least in my twisted mind, was to take it out on a golf course and shoot birdies at it.

Chasing is the sickest and most desperate element in compulsive gambling, going after unmanageable losses with even more money and greater risk. We would both do it.

This was my most daring, and irrational, chase. I was looking right down the throat of my real estate portfolio!

Looking back on North Carolina, I had not been beaten badly if only the golfing part of the outing was taken into consideration. I wasn't so far in the hole because of day-after-day of horrible drives, chips and putts. I had been destroyed by out of control gambling at the worst of times.

Consider, for example, that I was $25,000 ahead after 18 holes on the final day. I was feeling secure, probably artificially so, because my money was not at risk. That's only the natural way to feel when the other guy is trying to chase his own money and win it back.

That feeling of security turned out to be a dangerous state of mind. M.J. started revving up the stakes and I had no problem with that. Let him go for it. I felt like a baseball team with two weeks left in the season and the so-called magic number at one. There wasn't any way I was going to lose. Even if I did, I couldn't drop too much with that kind of a cushion.

Obviously, I wasn't doing a very good job of tracking where the numbers were headed. I had lost a sense of reality and gotten swept away by the euphoria of the risk. And then I got buried on that 45th hole when a most treacherous putt did not find its way home.

Given my state of mind and the insane decision I had made, I had to get out on the back deck and pound balls into the canyon. I practiced for hours and hours and hours. I was surprised the canyon did not turn white with golf balls the size of hail, if you get my twist.

Michael, meanwhile, was in the Bahamas. I don't know if he was down there for vacation or business, but I knew his golf clubs were not getting dusty in some closet. Knowing him, he surely sought out a high stakes opponent or two to keep his juices flowing. He has to have that.

———

When M.J. arrived in San Diego in September of 1991, I was ready with my game and ready with my proposal.

I knew there was no way he would refuse my proposal. In fact, I knew he would jump at it.

Jordan was staying at the La Costa Resort so I picked him up on the way to our game. We would be playing 36 holes, the first 18 at Pala Mesa and the second 18 at Pauma Valley, two nice courses in pretty inland valleys in the northern part of the county.

When Michael called the night before, he had asked about setting the game. We always played even so we didn't need to go through the ritualistic negotiation for strokes on the first tee. We only had to set the stakes and we had gotten so we did that in advance, at least for the morning round.

"I'll tell you what, M.J.," I said. "I'll have a proposal for you when I pick you up."

I was sure the mystery piqued his interest and that was exactly what I had in mind. He knew he had that $98,000 cushion. He had to be wondering what I was thinking.

M.J. settled comfortably into the passenger seat in my Jag. I don't want to sound like a commercial, but his 6-foot, 6-inch frame wasn't squeezed at all. He was fiddling with some of my R&B and funk tapes and trying to act disinterested, but I knew he was anxious to hear my proposal.

"OK, M.J., here's a check for $98,000," I said.

He took it and looked at me quizzically.

"Here's another check for $98,000," I said. "We'll play 36 holes today for these checks. If I win, I tear up the checks. If you win, you keep them."

"You sure?" he asked.

That was a damned good question. I was coming to him boldly and brashly, as though this little matter of tossing $196,000 on the line was something I did every day. In truth, I should have won an Oscar for my performance, which was quintessential false bravado.

"That's the game I want," I said. "You want it?"

"You're on," he said. "As long as you're sure you want to do it."

"I'm sure," I said. "What about Adolph's money? I have a check for him too."

Adolph wasn't there. Yet.

"He's in," M.J. said.

This confirmed what Adolph had told me earlier in the week, that he was still riding his horse. I could wipe out what I owed him too...or I could take even more of a beating.

It was a very nervous drive to Pala Mesa.

———

You want to talk suicidal? I was standing on the first tee at Pala Mesa. I had two $98,000 checks plus another for Adolph's $20,000 sitting on the console of my car. My nerves were as taut as guitar strings. I was from here to the moon out of my comfort zone. It was like my body was charged with electricity.

And I was teeing up to hit my second shot. I had hooked my first drive out of bounds, and we weren't playing mulligans. The first hole was a total disaster. I scored a triple bogey eight.

The second hole was no better. I scored another triple bogey after *again* hitting my first shot out of bounds. They don't make an anti-perspirant strong enough to stem the tide flowing from my hands and forehead. I was such a nervous fucking wreck my stomach felt like I had swallowed lava. Mark Etue was playing with us and he couldn't have had a clue the dilemma I was in.

Why had I done such a stupid thing? Why had I chased the whole debt at once? Why hadn't I done the sensible thing and tried to nibble away at it?

Why?

Because I was desperate and irrational.

There's no other explanation. Ah, my shrinking real estate holdings . . .

"Hey man," M.J. said, "you aren't giving up, are you?"

"Don't count me out," I mumbled.

"You know I don't take you lightly," he said.

Freddy Sarno has described my game as being volatile, like me, and prone to drastic and dramatic swings. I could be very good or very bad within the same round, and I had certainly gotten some very bad behind on those first two holes.

It has always been a characteristic of my game that I don't play even keel. It's a lot worse to shoot six bogeys and be six over par than two triple bogeys. The reason is that you have a chance to lose six holes with six bogeys, but only two holes with two triples. From a betting standpoint, you're better off with more holes played at even par.

I knew all this, but I was still very shaken as I went to the third tee. I always beat him when I drove well off the tee, and I had started with two horrendous drives. I usually play well when I get off to a good start and shitty when I start poorly. I needed to reach down and regroup...quickly.

Naturally, I was hitting last off the third tee. I took the opportunity while the others hit to indulge in a brief two-minute, eye closing TM session and gather my thoughts. I took a slug of my brain food. I did pranayama, a breathing exercise associated with yoga. I just needed to gather myself.

My sci-fi driver came back with a vengeance on the third tee. It took me long, well over 300 yards, and it took me straight on an uphill par-five. And it lifted me out of my doldrums.

All I had left was a three-iron, which wasn't much to have to hit as a second shot on a par-five. I knocked it 25 feet from the pin. Michael hadn't counted me out and I hadn't given up. With tremendous satisfaction, not to mention great effort at controlling my nerve endings, I made the putt for an eagle. I actually let loose with a yelp of enthusiasm which caught everyone off guard.

The eagle gave me an unbelievable psychological swing. I knew I was ready to roll. I had gotten a hole back and I had gotten two shots back, so the swing was much more than psychological.

After that nervous start, when I'm thinking Jordan's going to end up owning my cabin, I played one of the greatest rounds of my life. I played the next 15 holes in one over par. By the time we got to the 18th hole, I had the match won and I needed only a par to win the medal bet as well. I got my par and had a leg up on both match and medal play going to the afternoon round at Pauma Valley.

I was feeling much more confident on the 20-minute drive from Pala Mesa to Pauma Valley. I certainly wasn't about to let myself get overly secure, but the turnaround from those back-to-back triple bogeys put me into position to erase the debt which had nagged me since North Carolina.

Maybe I was going to get away with doing something stupid in the throes of desperation.

I didn't know much about Pauma Valley, just that John Delorean lived there and hung out when his world fell apart. I had never played the course, so it was intriguing. M.J. hadn't played it either, so we were on what might be called neutral turf. It was a tough course with a steep slope rating, like 77. We played with Etue and a member he knew, neither of whom could have realized the magnitude of the money involved. I needed to keep the lead I had established at Pala Mesa to hold onto those $98,000 checks.

Surprisingly, I was calm on the first tee. I played the first six holes in even par and M.J. was struggling. My drives were tremendous. I must have been out at least 300 yards on 10 of the 14 driving holes, the others, of course, being shorter par-threes.

I went out and shot a 75 from the blue tees, the championship tees. I was in control of the match right from the start. I was never in position where there was a critical shot I had to make. It didn't even hurt me when I hit a shot out of bounds on the 16th and had to take a double bogey.

The 18th hole was totally anti-climactic. We were playing for the checks on the console, so there weren't presses flying back and forth to complicate where we stood. I had him beaten and beaten badly. I didn't need the birdie I scored on the 18th, but it was a nice way to end a more than satisfying day.

During the drive back to La Costa, the checks just sat on the console of my Jag. M.J. hardly acknowledged their presence. They no longer existed as far as he was concerned. I didn't grab them and stuff them in my pocket or anything. I just let them sit. We didn't trash talk after a match. That day's winner was always respectful of that day's loser. He had been courteous to me when he had beaten me in North Carolina.

From M.J.'s point of view, it had not been a risky venture. None of his money had been at stake. His past earnings and future comfort had not been imperiled, as mine had.

When I dropped him off at La Costa, I waved good-bye and drove calmly away. I was as emotional as a sphinx, as far as Michael was going to see.

Once I was around a corner and out of sight, I let out a whoop and clenched my fist. I gave myself a high-five in the rear view mirror. I had done the daring. I had shown him my money. I had risked double what I owed him. I had made good. I had chased and won.

I had wiped the slate clean. I was elated. I was literally screaming and hollering. I was pounding the steering wheel.

What a rush! As I turned south on Interstate-5, I had an irresistible whim. I grabbed the envelopes and pulled the checks out. I tore them up and tossed the bits and pieces out the window. They were strewn for 30 miles along the freeway.

In a way, I had won more than $200,000. I had won it because I hadn't lost it.

I couldn't have known it at the time, but I was about to have a week like no other golfer in history. Eat your hearts out Jack and Arnie.

———

Our next stop, on a Saturday, was Aviara. This is an open course with over-sized greens created by a mistake in the drawings. The greens weren't drawn to scale so Aviara ended up characterized by its huge putting surfaces. You'd get onto a green and laugh about whether you had enough club to get the ball to the hole.

Now that we were back to even, we cut back on the numbers... at least a little bit. We had scheduled 36 holes, with a $25,000 match bet and $25,000 medal bet on each 18. Add that up and it still comes out to $100,000 potentially at risk, if one of us really buries the other guy. Essentially, we were a whole lot crazier than we had been in 1989 and most of 1990, but it wasn't like more than $200,000 of my money was lying on the console of the Jag.

Etue was playing with us again and we all had some smaller bets. I was relaxed and feeling good about my game.

I beat Michael three ways and pushed on the other one. Now I was up $75,000. That represents damned near a $300,000 swing over two days of golf. I was feeling very, very good about this wonderful twist of debt from my shoulders to Michael's.

M.J. had business in Portland, I assumed a board meeting with Nike, so we missed playing Sunday. That was fine because I had a scheduled brunch with owner Don Sterling and his Los Angeles Clippers, who were about to open training camp. I was lucky to get a chance to visit with the legendary Elgin Baylor, the general manager. The Clippers were opening a little ahead of the Bulls, but then they probably needed more practice.

We went the other direction Monday, down to Steel Canyon in the southeastern part of the county. It's a new course, short and tricky. The trees are small and young, but there are plenty of places to get into trouble.

This was another 36-hole day, this time with Freddy Sarno along. We had the same bets we had at Aviara. We had obviously accelerated our gambling and the result was an increase in pressure on every swing on every hole. Our level of psychic energy was soaring, at least mine was. The intensity was heating up ferociously. I was trying to concentrate on my breathing routine, muscle awareness and thought processes.

Typical of the day was the last hole of our first round, when I made a birdie and he made a seven or eight. His golf was deteriorating. All I had to do was manage my game and I was going to beat him. I could make low risk shots and rev my game down. Sometimes in golf, you get into a position where you have to make a great shot, an exceptional recovery shot or a big putt or a long drive. I never had to make a great shot. He couldn't tool up to my level. He was beating himself.

I made a minor gain on our running tab, like $18,000. Presses and side bets skewed it from the multiples of $25,000 we had at stake. Notice that $18,000 was now considered minor money, a nudge like maybe gaining one-eighth of a dollar a share on the stock market. Way back at Stardust that August morning in 1989, we had started this rivalry with a five-way wager for $500 each.

After our round at Steel Canyon, I was ahead $93,000. My stock was going up nicely.

Earlier, in a casual conversation about Adolph, I had told M.J. that his buddy was my worst nightmare and I didn't want him around me on the golf course. That statement was about to haunt me.

My telephone rang late that Monday night and it was Adolph.

"I just wanted you to know," he chortled, "that your worst fucking nightmare is in town."

He quoted back to me what I had told M.J., so I know they had gamesmanship strategy coming right at me.

"Great," I said, "but I don't want you to talk to me on the golf course. I don't care what else you do. Hang out, but don't fuck with me on the course. We'll talk after rounds, fine, and we'll be friends. But I'm trying to stay focused while I'm on the course and I don't want to listen to your shit."

I know damned well Michael flew him in as a tool to try to distract me. He would think that was cute and fun, especially after my statement about Adolph being my worst fucking nightmare. Now I was realizing that Jordan would do absolutely everything he could to win, including importing his homeboy to try to disrupt my focus. This exemplified their unique co-dependence, M.J. needing Adolph as much as vice versa.

I hung up the phone and cursed.

"You won't believe who that was," I told Kerry. "M.J. flew that bastard Adolph into town. I'm going to kick both their asses."

I wasn't the only one who didn't care for Adolph's presence

on the golf course. I was sitting with Freddy Sarno and Ron Heitzinger in the spring of 1990 talking about our upcoming games with Jordan when those guys came up with a complaint which didn't surprise me.

"You tell Michael I don't want any of his buddies following us around," Ron said. "I don't need distractions like Adolph when I'm trying to stay focused."

"Same for me," Freddy said. "Fred's a pretty classy guy, but Adolph's a pain in the ass. I just don't need that entourage breaking up my concentration. Those guys trying to make bets on this and that can get to be a nuisance."

We had no luck keeping Adolph away from our golf games. None at all.

And now, with the numbers getting outrageous, Adolph was on his way...again. My business intruded on Tuesday, so we were limited to 18 holes in the afternoon at The Farms. This was that elite private club in the Rancho Santa Fe area which had wooed me to become a member and then rejected my application. I still liked to play there and Michael was a member by 1991.

I went to the 18th hole in position to tack substantial numbers onto that $93,000 tab. I had a two shot lead, but I blew it. I hit two shots out of bounds and ended up with an eight on a par-five hole. The thing about that eight was that it would have been a birdie if I hadn't taken the penalty strokes for going O.B. What was actually my second swing got me onto the green from 245 yards away and I two-putted. Fortunately, M.J. had a six. He could have turned all the numbers around with a par, so my big approach shot helped me a lot by throwing some added pressure onto him. We ended up even and the tab was still $93,000.

We were back on The Farms Wednesday for 36 holes, once again joined by Mark Etue. I had some ups and downs, but I was never in danger of losing any money.

I'm in a zone. I'm playing "A" golf, my game fine-tuned and

tweaked. I'm making birdies and hitting good shots and everything is clicking. I'm shooting every round between 74 and 77
and suddenly Michael is having trouble breaking 80.

I won $60,000 and the tab hit $153,000. This was the highest
either one of us had gone in terms of debt owed. We had played
that day for my two $98,000 checks, but that didn't represent
debt owed. It could well have represented money lost, but I
dodged the bullet on that one.

———

"M.J.," I said, "we do not have to keep playing for this kind
of money."

I was concerned where we might be headed. I had gotten
out of control with those checks on the line and the numbers
were now going up again, albeit they were now in my favor.

"Listen," I said, "I'm willing to discount this thing right now
and get out of this thing and get back to sensible numbers. How
about it?"

I was kicking his ass. My game was chiseled and his was
falling apart. Adolph's distracting presence was not even
helping and I was starting to enjoy the fact that he was there to
watch. You get your ass kicked like that on a basketball court,
you call a time-out and try to regroup.

"No," he said. "Let's keep playing. I gave you a chance so
you've gotta give me a chance."

"OK," I said. "I guess that's only fair. But I'm serious about
not wanting to wager at this level. We really don't need this."

This plea was made frequently. I guess if I was really serious
I would have walked off, but when a golfer is asking for a
chance to win money back you feel obligated. And, he gave me
a chance and was quick to remind me.

He wanted me to reciprocate and I felt obligated because
he had given me that chance after I lost the $98,000 in North
Carolina.

Back on The Farms on Thursday, Michael came up with an absolutely outlandish proposal. He wanted to play 18 holes with $80,000 on the match bet and $80,000 on the medal bet. That was $160,000 at stake. He came up with that figure because he was trying to rev the pressure, put me in a position where I could win and be up $313,000 or lose and suddenly be $7,000 down.

We were loading in our carts when he came forward with his proposal.

"E-Man," he said, "I want to do more than get even. I want you to owe me."

That was savvy, trying to plant discomfort in my psyche. That was gamesmanship.

I was not going to cave in. The funny thing about this round was that we played with Hank Egan and Jim Brandenburg. Egan, M.J.'s partner, was basketball coach at the University of San Diego and Brandenburg, my partner, was basketball coach at San Diego State. This was a rare "public relations" round, which Michael didn't usually like, but these were basketball guys and he didn't complain. I was pushing our intra-city championship basketball game between San Diego's two major universities at the Sports Arena, and I thought it would be a nice perk to get these guys out on a golf course with M.J. I hadn't realized what the stakes would be when I invited them to play.

What was funny? In our partnership game, the bet was $2 three ways. How's that for a study in contrasts?

I don't think Brandenburg and Egan had a clue what was at stake in our game, other than the fact that we weren't doing a lot of bantering back and forth. I suppose they had to sense the tension. We had given them the usual prompting about never knocking putts away because Michael and I had a separate game.

Michael managed to get his game together, at least for awhile, and he had me down the first six holes. However, I was just playing too well for it to last. I finished the front nine birdie, par, birdie.

"Attaboy," Brandenburg said, patting me on the back after No. 9 like I was one of his basketball players. "You got him now."

He was right. I ended up having a tremendous day and kicked his ass again, getting birdies on Nos. 15 and 18 to put it away.

When we finished, Michael was courteous to Egan and Brandenburg as they departed but I could tell he was preoccupied and stressed. After all, he was now down $313,000.

The coaches had hardly cleared the parking lot when he snapped: "We're going to play nine more holes for the $313,000. Come on, E-Man, we've got time."

He was pissed at himself and disgruntled. He's a competitor and he was getting his ass kicked. He hadn't had this kind of a beating on the basketball court or in life. He has this whole different mentality on losing. He can't stand to lose. I was now seeing an almost psycho level of competitiveness.

I am really not liking this, no matter that I am the one on the long end of the tab.

"Michael," I pleaded, "I'm not here to hustle you for this kind of money. This is getting to be ridiculous. Where's it going to stop?"

He came back at me once again with his argument about reciprocating a chance to get even. He tightened the screws and insisted that I was obligated to give him this chance...to allow him to engage in this chase.

"Listen," I said, "I'll let you out right now. I'll negotiate a settlement. You're insisting on playing. If we continue to play, you know I expect that you are going to pay if you lose."

My pleas were from my heart. It did not make any sense to keep revving it up. I thought if he knew I was serious about payment he would be inclined to settle.

"Relative to our comparative wealth," he said, "the $98,000 you lost to me was a lot more than $313,000 is to me."

"You may be right, Michael," I said, "but these numbers are ridiculous."

We went back out onto the course for nine more holes in the gathering darkness. The sprinklers were coming on but we played through them.

I kicked his butt. I shot a 37 with two birdies, a bogey and a double bogey. M.J. shot a 42 or 43.

The number, his debt to me, was at $626,000.

———

"This is way beyond fucking limits," I told him. "Let's get out of this insanity. Let's work a way."

I was getting heated up and pissed off that we were betting at such a level. He was getting cooked up and outraged. He was flustered that he was losing and I was frustrated that I couldn't seem to get inside his bald head and get his attention. I felt trapped in a surreal world and I couldn't get out. I wanted help, but there was nowhere to go.

M.J. was irrational. It was almost as if he wasn't seeing Richard Esquinas any more. He was seeing me as someone like a Bill Laimbeer, a hated and serious adversary from the Detroit Pistons. I was like all of the Pistons in one body. The tension was tremendous and I could feel his frustration building.

I was backing off putts because there was so much pressure I couldn't grip the club, and I was ahead.

A real hustler, a cold-heartedly calculating gambler, would have gone for the kill in this situation and thrown friendship to the wind. This would have been the moment to rev it up and put him away. I knew his game at that point in time couldn't come close to mine. I was playing too well and he was strug-gling.

I was honestly thinking to myself that there had to be a way to call a halt. I could get a hard-on playing for $5,000 or $10,000. I didn't need or want numbers like we had reached to give me a rush. It had gone beyond even being fun, there was so much pressure on every swing, every step, every word. Our verbal exchanges became terse and unfriendly. The human nervous system was not built to absorb such pulsating intensity.

We had slid from a friendship thing to an adversarial thing. I was not comfortable with where our golf had taken us or what it had turned us into.

———

On the way back to his hotel, we had a long conversation. He wanted to keep on going, double it up again. I was virtually begging for sanity.

"I want to just settle this thing and get back to reasonable bets," I told him. "I can see where it's taxing our friendship. I can see it deteriorating. I don't like it."

"No way this will hurt our friendship," he said.

My therapist later explained to me that a relationship such as this is a love affair of sorts. It's not a sexual thing, of course, but rather a matter of two individuals sharing the mood-altering rush of a challenge which boiled their juices. If that was the case, I guess we were having a real orgy.

He had not convinced me that the situation was not impacting our friendship, partially because he was so defensive in the way that he said it.

The conversation, from his side anyway, kept coming back to going double or nothing.

"Michael, are you prepared to pay $1.2 million?" I asked impatiently. "I'm doing my best to get the fuck out of this and you want to keep doubling up. You put me in that situation, and I'm going to want to win. Would you rather I drop my hands and let you win?"

This riled him. I hadn't meant to piss him off, but I did. In retrospect, I had hit at the heart of his ego. Here I was, asking him if he would be happier if I just let him win to put a wrap on the whole crazy thing.

In truth, there was no way I could have let him win. I had worked my ass off to get where I was with the numbers. I had taken a gigantic gamble and come away clean. I was beating him fair and square. More importantly, I was earnestly offering him settlements which would get us out of the insanity and back to reasonable levels.

Once again, M.J. went into a long story about his wealth. He could handle $1.2 million, he said, should he happen to lose.

"Let's play for it," he said. "E-Man, I can't believe you won't give me this game."

I was trying to get him to comprehend the magnitude of losing at such a level, to defer this insistence that we engage once again. Not only did he want to continue this chase, he was demanding it.

"I do not want this game," I said, "but I must be honest with you. You lose and you pay. That's the only way I'll give you a shot. And, if I beat you, that's it. No more of this double or nothing shit."

———

Little did my buddies at Aviara realize that their course was to be the site of perhaps the richest single one-on-one round in the history of golf. The date was September 20, 1991.

The touring pros never play with $1.25 million on the line for an individual to win, not even in the skins games. If a professional tournament features a $1.25 million prize, the winner gets $225,000 and the remainder is divided from second through 70th place. And those guys have to work for four days.

Michael was never in the match. I parred the first hole and M.J. bogeyed. I had a sense of being in control as we walked from the green to the cart.

More of the same followed. I parred the second hole and

Michael double-bogeyed. M.J. rallied a bit with a par to my bogey on No. 3. That was his last hurrah.

On the par-four ninth hole, I almost drove the green. I chipped up and one-putted and I was three holes ahead with nine to play. We were playing our usual match/medal combo, this $313,000 match and $313,000 medal with some side bets on birdies.

After I closed him out on the 17th, the 18th was anti-climactic except for the smaller bets with Etue. Michael and Adolph virtually raced down the 18th fairway because it was a meaningless hole.

M.J.'s game had deserted him. I don't think it was the pressure, but that could have been a factor. I didn't think the pressure would bother a guy who had been in as many big games as he had on the basketball court. But then, basketball came naturally to him and golf didn't.

Michael Jordan was down $1.252 million to me. He was in a hurry to leave because he had to get to Chicago for a fund-raising event for his Michael Jordan Foundation. And this was also the weekend the 1992 U.S. Olympic basketball team—the Dream Team—was being introduced. His plane was waiting.

After the 18th hole, he said: "You're gonna be in Hilton Head. We'll settle after we're done there."

"Christ, M.J., I expect at least a partial payment after a week like this," I told him. "We've already set the table and this was the premise of all of our long conversations."

He wanted one more chance.

"Michael, we've had this conversation," I said. "We're out of here. We're off the charts. I want something today, even if it's only $50,000. That's what we agreed. We'd play if you'd pay. I'll negotiate down right now to $500,000 if you want to pay."

"I'll send you a check for $50,000," he said. "We'll play the rest at Hilton Head. I gave you time now I'm asking you for time."

"GQ," Adolph interrupted, "there ain't no way you're gonna get paid."

"Fuck you, Adolph," I said. "This is none of your business."

M.J. said: "Adolph, get into the car."

I was frosted. I was starting to feel the sickness of gambling. It was hitting me over the head. I had played a guy who totally understood the stakes and the consequences, who insisted he was good for the debt, and now he was in a hurry to get out of town without as much as a partial payment.

"Gotta go," Jordan said.

"M.J.," I said, "this is not fair."

"I'll be in touch," he said. "Really E-Man, I'll make it right."

And he was gone...with Adolph.

———

I was invited to Hilton Head for his annual pre-training camp gathering, which I had made in 1989 and 1990. I was dying to go, but I was president of the San Diego Gulls and the hockey season was starting. I also had continuing negotiations regarding the tentative sale of the Sports Arena.

Michael had been busy too. He had had to go to North Carolina for the dedication of the freeway named in his honor and then on to New York for an appearance on "Saturday Night Live."

However, he was in need of that last golfing and gambling fling before the basketball season started.

M.J. called me and Adolph called me and they were almost begging me to break away and come back. They put on a full-court press with numerous calls, but I just couldn't responsibly break away.

Jordan was even getting more sensible about the stakes, if you consider $100,000 on a medal bet and $100,000 on a match bet to be sensible.

"We'll play for that," he said, "and see where we are at the end of the week. Then I'll settle."

I wanted M.J. to have time, but I never really thought he would start the dodging, the avoiding, the denying process so promptly after our hoopla at Aviara.

The day I was supposed to arrive in Hilton Head was the day before the Chicago Bulls were supposed to visit President Bush in the White House. Had I been able to make it, I would have been on the golf course with Jordan the day he stiffed the President. He still didn't bother going to the White House, of course. How could he? There were golf courses open in Hilton Head.

Chapter Twelve

My Cry For Help

Hugh Stephenson was curious about my golf game. He was curious about whether I was stimulated by the challenge of the game itself or by external factors, such as the stakes involved. I knew what he was saying and I knew he probably already knew the answer.

"Does golf give you a kick?" he asked. "Does it give you a charge?"

"I enjoy it," I said, "but I don't get any gratification out of playing golf if there isn't some action. I'm not a leisurely golfer. I don't play golf to hang out and look at the trees. That's not me."

Trees? The only way I would notice them was if I was in them. And that's no place to be with a golf ball on the ground and a stick in your hand. Trees are trouble. I didn't pay much attention to the songs of the birds or the smells of the flowers either.

Golf was serious fun to me, particularly at the levels Jordan and I had reached in our betting.

Let me put this in perspective. How many people go to the race track because they want to look at the horses? Not many, right? Take the pari-mutuel windows out of a thoroughbred track and not many people would be in the stands, regardless of what purists might argue.

"You're addicted to gambling," my therapist, Lori Stephenson, had told me.

"Money has to be part of it for you," Hugh said.

I hired Dr. Hugh Stephenson, a clinical psychologist, as a consultant in March of 1993. He had done considerable research on gambling as an addiction and I asked him to enlighten me more on gambling as an epidemic.

Naturally, he became interested in my personal situation as well, it being rather unique in the magnitude of my wagering with M.J. The Stephensons are married, but they practice separately and dealt with me on different levels at different times.

I didn't have to talk for very long before both were convinced I was addicted to gambling, though I continued to insist my addiction was limited to the golf course. I was stubbornly maintaining that I wanted to *control* my gambling rather than stop it altogether.

I didn't want to find myself laying $216,000 in checks on a dashboard and heading for the first tee. I didn't want to find myself playing M.J. for $616,000 of his money, double or nothing.

That was stupid. That had to stop.

What had happened to me?

What had happened to Michael?

━━━

I was sitting on a couch and Hugh was sitting nearby. I was tapping his strong background in treating adolescents and adults with addictive personalities. He had a legal pad scrawled with notations from his up-to-the-minute research on gambling as an addiction. I was about to get a primer.

"Marijuana was the addiction of the 60s," Hugh explained, "heroin the 70s, cocaine the 80s and, from my research of an article in the "Utne Reader" by Robert McClory, gambling is the addiction of the 90s."

I never touched any of that other stuff. It was all foreign to me. I don't even drink, except maybe an occasional champagne toast. I don't smoke. I'm a 90s man. I gamble.

Hugh was talking and I was listening. I liked both of these people right away. I never asked their ages, but they are probably about the same as me. Probably in their mid 30s. They were serious without being stodgy, like you picture a shrink might be from watching movies. They have good senses of humor, which was a must in dealing with me and my irreverence.

"Estimates from 1990 indicate $286 billion was circulated through gambling, legal and illegal," Hugh said. "That was $34 *billion* more than the year before. It's growing at 10 per cent a year in spite of the recession and everything else."

"Michael and I contributed a lot to the 10 per cent growth for '91, huh?" I laughed.

See what I mean about irreverence?

This was an interesting day to be talking about gambling because all of California was going berserk over the lottery. Convenience stores weren't very convenient, because the lottery had rolled over to $55 million and the places were packed with fortune hunters. You needed a quart of milk and you had to stand in line with people counting nickels out of their piggy banks.

The governmental support of gambling had not been lost on Hugh. The State of California was patting all these people on the back and telling them how good it was to gamble and how profitable it might be. There were billboards, television commercials and radio jingles. They had a promotion awhile back where you got a free deck of cards for three plays on Decco, one of the lottery games. Was that using one form of gambling to encourage another or what?

"People have become very comfortable with the lottery," Lori had told me. "It's gambling, but it has become psychologically acceptable. It has become such a part of our society that no one protests any more. They say look at the terrible shape of our roads and the terrible shape of our government and the terrible shape of our schools and then we're told taxes won't have to be raised if we legalize more gambling."

"It's a sin tax," Hugh said. "Profit from a vice."

There is the less-than-subliminal message that Californians cannot lose, because education was benefiting from the proceeds. I have always been skeptical of exactly how much money went to schools, particularly in light of the fact that schools seem to be cutting back more than ever on vital programs.

"Ten per cent of the players purchase 50 per cent of the tickets for the lottery," Hugh said, again citing McClory's article. "That's right. That small a group puts up that much of the money. Of that group, African-Americans and Hispanics are the vast majority of the ticket buyers. You're talking a small group of people, typically young people without much money to begin with, pumping a lot of money into the lottery."

These numbers staggered me. I could see exactly what he had been saying about compulsive gamblers. I wouldn't have been surprised if that same ratio, 10 per cent betting more than 50 per cent, was also true at horse tracks, Las Vegas and even illegal bookmakers. It made sense. I wouldn't be surprised if 10 per cent of the population drinks 50 per cent of the alcohol consumed.

Hugh was spouting more numbers from McClory, who cited a study by the National Institute of Mental Health. He said approximately 4.2 million Americans are addicted gamblers, 36 per cent of those women, 43 per cent non-white, eight per cent under 30 and 50 per cent with incomes under $25,000.

"The biggest recent surge," he said, "was among teenagers."

"What's their game of choice?" I wondered. "Craps?"

That had been how I had started, beating the black kid from down the street in Columbus out of $4 at dice.

"It has to do with the family atmosphere," Hugh said. "Dad,

the parents, whatever they bet. Horses. Football. Basketball. Friday night poker games."

"When Uncle Guido comes over?" I said.

"It's like alcohol or cigarettes in the house," he said, ignoring Uncle Guido. "Within the family framework, permission is being given at a very early age to do it."

My dad gambled later in life, after he had moved to California, but I don't recall any boyhood exposure. And his gambling seemed to be along the same vein as a lot of others, making one or two trips to Las Vegas. His quirk was that he would sit at the same slot machine until it paid off, regardless of whether he had to pour coins into it for 24 hours.

After he died, I found these numbers written in a book he had in his trailer in San Bernardino. It looked like he was working on a system for beating the California lottery. He had bought some tickets the day he died, but none of them paid off.

In truth, I'm not sure betting the lottery at such a modest level is a compulsion as much as a habit.

However, Hugh was right about my experience during my senior year at Ohio State.

"Gambling usually starts with small amounts at cards and then maybe $5, $10 or $20 on sports events," Hugh said. "It gets out of control when a kid gets to college or maybe out of college and he has more money to spend."

I was definitely betting beyond my means at OSU.

Hugh and other gambling experts have this theory that the biggest gambling center in the future will be the living room, which really brings it into the home. He says the technology is there. Maybe it will be in the form of a casino channel on the tube or a gaming program on the computer or an as-yet unidentified attachment to the telephone. Maybe I could play golf against a computer-generated opponent for heaven knows what stakes.

In the real world, such as it was given the money at stake in the Jordan matches, I qualified as being out of college with money to spend. However, I didn't have the money to spend that Michael Jordan had. In truth, M.J. still has it.

———

For all my sessions with Lori over all these months, so much of what she had to say hit home. I thought at first it was uncanny how well she knew me. I realized she didn't know me as much as she knew my type. Darned if Hugh didn't know me too. Of course, knowing my type was knowing me.

"The typical compulsive gambler's profile is that he is brighter than average," Hugh said. "The lottery doesn't take intelligence, but other forms of gambling do. The compulsive gambler is a tenacious achiever, a high achiever."

Lori walked in to gather some papers and overheard.

"You'll hear yourself here," she said.

"And they are tough competitors," Hugh said. "They also have exceptionally low thresholds of boredom. They have a high need for stimulation. It makes sense that someone who is highly competitive likes to take on big projects, big competitions, whatever."

This was fitting me so far. It was all over me.

"Compulsive gamblers also have a tendency to think money can solve anything," Hugh said. "They think enough money will cure everything, buy everything, solve everything."

He missed me here. I really don't have anything I am trying to cure or solve with money. I don't gamble in pursuit of the big score. I have a ton of equity in the La Jolla house and I own the Ohio cabin outright. I pay the credit cards monthly. The gambling with Jordan was more for the jousting, more for the hunt, more for the rush. I'm surely not saying it was not somewhere out beyond the edge, but I am trying to define my motivation.

Maybe I was missing the point here, taking things a little too personally. Hugh wasn't trying to apply every trait to me, but rather to educate me on what he had seen and observed.

Enough of it was hitting home. It didn't all have to be specific to my case.

"The gambler is seeking that high, that big win, the sound of money coming down," he continued. "That's what hooks people. It undermines the classic American work ethic, that you work hard for something, pay your dues, work hard, work hard, and you are rewarded. The crucial thing going on in America is that people are having trouble delaying gratification and working hard instead."

"Everyone wants to hit a home run?" I asked. "No one wants to hit singles?"

It's that big win, the sound of money coming down which causes people to go crazy when a state lottery gets up to something like $55 million. Slot machines and their modern video counterparts cause that same sensation. There isn't even an element of skill involved in this kind of gambling.

I suppose I have to concede that taking a couple hundred dollars worth of quarters to Las Vegas or plunking $25 worth of quick picks on a lottery is a little more sensible than the kind of stuff I was doing with M.J. The problem, as Hugh explained it, was some of the people making such modest bets were already beyond their means. Being out of control is a relative thing.

Referring to author John Bradshaw's definition in *Bradshaw On: The Family*, Hugh quoted directly from the book: "Compulsive/addictive behavior has a pathological relationship to any mood-altering experience that has life damaging consequences."

"Physical or mental?" I wondered.

"Ruining your family fortune, ruining your health, ruining your marriage," Hugh said. "Either or both physical and mental can be involved. The classic ones would be tobacco, alcohol and drugs. In this day and age, it has gone beyond the thinking that an addict is someone who's down and out and has to be a minority. More and more people on all socio-economic levels have compulsive addictive behaviors. The difference is that some compulsions are more socially acceptable. If you're a workaholic, your family may not like it, but you may be very successful in society's eyes."

———

Hugh and Lori Stephenson had some thoughts on sports gambling that opened my eyes. They changed my thinking a little bit on the Pete Rose situation, for example. They changed my way of thinking on Michael Jordan a lot.

They started talking about drugs. I am not even remotely suggesting that either Rose or Jordan was in any way involved with drugs. My experience with Jordan was that he rarely and barely indulged in alcohol and I have never heard Rose's name linked with a problem in that area. They were talking about drugs because they were talking about being beholding, and that would lead them to gambling.

"Fixing games always has been the big scandal," Hugh said. "Different regulatory agencies say they are cracking down, but I still think it's happening in many sports. A lot of athletes have a drug of choice, like cocaine has been the last 10 or 12 years. Get certain players addicted where they need lots of money and they get free drugs to throw two or three games a year. The danger is there because the habit is so insidious."

Just before this, Hugh had made the point that sports gambling is considered second only to drugs as a source of income for organized crime. I saw the connection between gambling and organized crime. That was obvious. However, I was having trouble tracking how both drugs and gambling had the potential to impact a player's performance in an area such as shaving points or throwing games.

Lori drove the point home.

"What could you be doing if you weren't you?" she asked. "You have told me that Michael owes you a million dollars."

"So you ask him to shave some points or throw a game or two," Hugh said. "Something you can bet on and get your money back."

It hit me right between the eyes.

"Or ask him to sit out a game," I said, "with something like a twisted ankle."

None of us were suggesting this is even a remote possibility with Michael, but the stark reality that such a scenario could happen with *someone* underscored to me why gambling has the potential to be such a cancer in the world of sports. This is merely an example of what *could* happen given the wrong people in a different circumstance. Michael and I *did not* fit here.

"You and Michael Jordan aren't the only ones gambling," Hugh said. "Gambling is rampant in American professional sports and America in general. It isn't just Michael and you."

———

Hugh does a lot of research, a lot of reading, on gambling. He came up with some facts compiled by the California Council on Compulsive Gambling.

"They are pretty eye-opening," he said. The Maryland State Task Force figured in 1990 that approximately 50,000 adult compulsive gamblers cost Maryland $1.5 billion—that's billion—through lost work productivity as well as money stolen and embezzled, bad checks and unpaid taxes. That's just one small state among 50.

Imagine what the cost analysis would be for California with roughly 300,000 adult compulsive gamblers and more than a million problem gamblers.

Approximately 40 per cent of all white collar crime is believed by the American Insurance Institute to be gambling related. Sixty-six per cent of all compulsive gamblers admit to committing crimes to pay their gambling debts and continue their gambling. About 20 per cent of all compulsive gamblers have attempted suicide.

The CCCG report, "The Cost of Compulsive Gambling," said: "The children of compulsive gamblers do worse in school than their peers, are more apt to have alcohol, drug or gambling problems and eating disorders and are more likely to be depressed. They attempt suicide twice as often as their classmates."

Hugh always amazed me—and shocked me—with his information on compulsive gambling.

———

Gambling, as an addiction, goes through an assortment of phases, as outlined very well by Clive Gammon in his *Sports Illustrated* article "Tales of Self-Destruction." Actually, gambling does not become an addiction, or can't be considered to be an addiction, if it stays in the very first stage.

The *social* phase.

Hugh was outlining these phases for me and I was listening, trying to understand where I fit.

"Most gamblers," he said, "stay at a social pace, play cards with their friends, bet a little money in the office pool, keep the stakes small. The social phase is where 80 per cent of the people are able to keep it. Maybe three to four per cent of those who gamble are compulsive gamblers, spending a lot of money, getting out of control and going for fast action casino and sports gambling."

The trigger, he said, is a big score. This is where they start thinking about gambling being a cure or a solution.

The *winning* phase.

Then comes the *losing* phase.

"They start betting on more things," Hugh said, "and they are not betting quite so rationally. They think they have a magic touch and they forget the odds are always against them. They will hit this losing phase. This is where it really becomes a problem. This is where it starts impacting family and friends because the gambler needs to borrow money to try to keep it going, or get it back together. They think they can win back what they have lost and they get deeper and deeper into a hole."

I was remembering when I had lost that $98,000 in North Carolina. I was thinking about coming home and refinancing the house or maybe mortgaging the cabin. That would qualify as borrowing to get even. That was certainly a losing phase in my golf games with M.J.

I just knew I could come up with what I needed. It would hurt, but I could make it happen.

"Gamblers," Hugh continued, "are usually very socially pleasant and attractive people. Good friends will trust them. You need a $1,000 and they'll lend you that kind of money. They probably won't even ask why you need it. They won't know you need it to bail out."

That, it turned out, was the next phase.

The *bailout* phase.

"Is Jordan in the bailout phase?" I asked.

"How much money does he owe other people?" Hugh said.

"I don't know," I said. "He's told me I'm his No. 1 adversary. I suppose there are others he owes $20,000 here and $100,000 there."

It was hard to pinpoint where Michael Jordan might be. It was easy to pinpoint where I had been.

Desperation is the final stage.

"That's where a gambler gets totally irrational," Hugh said. "He's almost delusional. He starts throwing money away."

I had done that, or at least tried to do that. I had written those $98,000 checks and handed them to M.J. He had tossed them onto the console of my car before we went out and played 36 holes of golf with those checks, my money, as stakes.

That was desperation.

And I knew M.J. had been there too.

"That's where he was during The Kill," I said, using my favorite nickname for that million dollar binge. "He wasn't playing well, but he was still doubling bets. I'm trying to get him out, but he won't listen to reason. His judgment was off and his game was off."

"I can't speak for Jordan's situation, of course, but you are describing the kind of *situation* where somebody needs in-patient treatment," Hugh said. "They need intervention like an alcoholic or a drug addict. You have to realize you've hit bottom and you're out of control."

"But you're irrational," Lori said.

"A lot of people are easy prey when they are in the desperation phase," Hugh said. "That's when the vultures move in. That's when they are vulnerable to the criminal element."

It's still a little bit difficult to assess exactly where Jordan fits in this equation, and I am certainly not being judgmental. He has always stressed to me his great wealth. When I was trying to talk him out of doubling $616,000 to $1.25 million, he argued that that kind of money to him was the same as $98,000 or maybe even $200,000 to me. He used that argument about his wealth a lot. He had insisted that we play and I had insisted that I would be paid if we played and I won.

Had he gone from the losing phase to the bailout phase to the desperation phase? Did his great wealth make him somehow immune to these phases? Where exactly might his comfort zone stop and panic start?

I was thinking of something Jim Brown, the former football star, had mentioned to me when I had dinner with him and my dear friend Mannie Jackson one night. We were talking, in general of course, about playing golf with Michael Jordan.

"Mark my word," he said in stern tones, "one day even Michael Jordan will get to a level where he can no longer pay."

Jim Brown could not possibly have known how that statement hit home, being M.J. owed me $1.25 million and I was having trouble collecting.

What I couldn't know was where Jordan might be with other losses. Newspapers and magazines had reported about investigations detailing possible losses in the Carolinas to a bail bondsman and a convicted drug dealer. There could well be others out there.

One thing was certain.

I was what might be called a safe opponent.

Because of my dealings with the San Diego Sports Arena, which was essentially a public trust, I had been thoroughly investigated by the city. My financial records were on file. My background had been checked. I didn't have any skeletons which would come out of the closet and rattle Jordan's image. The NBA could not call him in and upbraid him for associating with a person such as I.

"You were the right person to play with," Lori had told me. "You're clean. You have a high profile image. You're seen very positively in your community."

I wasn't a risk, not like those other guys who surfaced. For heaven's sake, one of them had three checks from Jordan totalling $108,000 in the trunk of his car. This guy had been shot to death.

"He saw that in the games I made we were playing with solid citizens," I told Lori earlier. "He saw me at basketball games, who I was with, where I was sitting, at mid-court, and it was sending him comfort signals that he could joust with me at the level we were at."

"There are only certain people you can bet with like that," Hugh said. "Only certain people have the money, know how to play the game and are into high stakes. You both, on some level, picked each other out."

"It's like the backgammon circuit," I said. "Believe me, all the money players know who they are. It's a closed shop. The big players can pick each other out like they have homing devices."

Jordan and I have met through a third party, of course. Smokey Gaines had introduced us at the post-game party following our 1989 All-Star game at the Sports Arena. Smokey had touted my game, I know, and my respectability, I presume.

"Then," I said, "you lay the bravado on top of that. It goes right to the weakness of a gambler. Ching. Ching."

Bravado is part of it. Hugh had called it machismo. M.J. and I had talked trash on that first tee at Stardust the very first day we played. I had talked trash just challenging him to be there. And he had asked me if I might be intimidated just being on the golf course with him.

"That type of posturing," Hugh said, "is typical of gamblers. It's the swagger. It's the talking big. It's the heart of their self-esteem."

That sounds like a profile of athletes as well as gamblers. They all posture and swagger. They all ooze with self-esteem. They thrive on all this, which might, in summation, be called ego. And their egos are constantly fed and reinforced.

"Take away that ability and are they still somebody?" asked Hugh.

"That's what they have to contend with when their careers are over," I answered. "It's a shock for them. Their audience is gone."

It was significant, I was learning, that Jordan chose to take me on in an alternative sport. It was another venue for testing himself. He could test himself at stakes which were high at their most modest levels and outlandish as we slid out of control.

━━━

Gamblers Anonymous, Hugh informed me, has approximately 12,000 members in 800 chapters in the U.S. That seemed an absurdly small number of people seeking help for a problem I was being told was so prevalent.

"There you go," Lori said. "It's not seen as a problem."

I see a problem. I see the Stephensons. I seek help. I can't say for sure exactly where I am, but I am reaching out and looking. In therapy, at GA, and through this book.

I also reach out to Michael Jordan, my friend and adversary.

I had read some of the things M.J. said when those checks, for $100,000 or whatever, have come up. He apologized that he was naive, and I don't really think Michael Jordan is naive. Compulsive gamblers are very sharp, very bright, street smart. It's damage control when he says he didn't know who he was associating with. He didn't know so-and-so was a drug dealer, and I am certain that's true. He says he apologizes, that he should have been smarter. He says he's sorry if he hurt anybody. But I've never heard him say he has a problem and he's trying to do something about it. Never.

To me, that's denial.

"That sounds like classic denial," Hugh responded. "Denial is so classic among addicts of any kind that you can't handle it with words. You need a sledgehammer. The bigger the person, the tougher it's going to be to crack them. They have too many people telling them how wonderful they are."

I went to the library and checked the computer for stories in which Michael Jordan's name appeared as a principal subject of stories or columns. It was an interesting study in contrasts. There were columns describing him as perhaps the greatest basketball player ever and extolling the virtues of his play against Cleveland or Portland or Detroit or Los Angeles. And there were stories reporting alleged gambling activities and decrying his lost credibility and endangered image.

Essentially, it appeared to me his athletic image and his personal image were getting to be at odds with one another.

I wondered if he was paying attention.

Even should a compulsive gambler recognize his or her problem, there are ramifications neither therapy nor Gamblers Anonymous can cure.

Debts.

"You may still owe a lot of money," Hugh said, "and you're going to still have people badgering you to pay up. You can't just say you're sorry, that you are going to meetings or undergoing therapy or both."

I can see where that wouldn't work. You owe some thug $300,000 (or even $5,000) and he is not going to be interested in this cleansing experience, this going to meetings, because all he wants cleansed is the debt. GA, in fact, encourages restitution.

Michael Jordan had incurred this debt to me, but I was no thug. I was not going to ask him to toss a few games so I could get some major bets down in Las Vegas. I was not going to threaten to send some ape to break his multi-million dollar legs.

I'm not going to tell you I would not like to be paid.

I just wonder if he thinks the same rules that apply to everyone else don't apply to him. Maybe he's thinking he's Michael Jordan, so I can wait for him.

"He says he wants to stay friends with me," I said. "He plays on the friendship thing. There's the value of friendship and the value of money..."

After all, we did engage in betting, both of us. Nobody twisted our arms. If anything, I twisted everything *but* his arms trying to get him to stop. We both played and he kept doing the bet and he lost the bet. He has a responsibility to do what he made a "contract" to do by insisting we continue, but he hasn't done that. If anyone has sullied the friendship, it's M.J.

"You're trying to use rational methods to understand your predicament," Hugh said, "but it sounds like it is out of control."

I am beginning to understand myself. I am not understanding Michael Jordan. That gives us something else we have in common. I'm not sure Michael Jordan understands himself either.

Chapter Thirteen

The Aftermath

"Michael," I said, "this is ridiculous. You've gotta give me some payment. You owe me $1.25 million and you haven't paid me a cent."

It was ridiculous that we had played a game of golf for such an outrageous amount of money. Sure it was. No doubt about it.

Gambling can be a terrible addiction. One more roll of the dice or one more deal of the cards is all it takes to turn a nasty world good or a good world nasty. The danger is part of the gambler's psyche.

Michael Jordan and I had gone completely over the edge in 1991 when we allowed our betting to build to that $1.25 million debt. We got there because I successfully chased my $98,000 debt and Michael unsuccessfully chased his debt as it climbed into seven figures.

Did he want to play for double or nothing on the $1.25 million? I presume he would have played double or nothing forever, or at least until he won. The tab could go to $2.5 million and $5 million and $10 million and then onward to match the national debt.

I called a halt at $1.25 million. I told him before we played that double or nothing match for $626,000 that we would be even if he won but that he would have to pay me if I won. I had begged him to deal with the $626,000 and negotiate a reasonable payoff, but he had insisted on playing. I told him that would be it. I told him so clearly there was no way he could have misunderstood.

Now I was standing in the kitchen of his Chicago home late in the 1991-92 NBA season. The night before I was in town to watch a late March game against the Cleveland Cavaliers. I sat with his lovely wife Juanita and we joined the Chicago Bears' Richard Dent and his wife for dinner after the game. The debt and what to do about it had come up as we were watching my alma mater, Ohio State, play Michigan in an NCAA Tournament game on television in the other room.

The conversation had started almost nonchalantly, at least from his standpoint. It was almost as if it was no big deal, that the debt would go away. Or that maybe I would break down and keep playing him double or nothing until he won and his debt was nothing once again.

The Ohio State-Michigan game went into overtime and we adjourned to the kitchen to get something to drink.

I was getting pissed at his attitude and the conversation went from intense to heated.

"You said you were going to send some money in September when you got back here," I said, "but you've ignored the whole thing."

"You have to give me some space," he said. "You have to give me some time. I've got these other things to deal with."

These "other things" were those reports that he had incurred substantial gambling losses in other forays through the Carolinas. He was getting subpoenas to testify in trials. And he was being called on the carpet by the NBA. He was in the kitchen and feeling the heat.

M.J. had suspected since the previous fall that his gambling losses to a hustler named James (Slim) Bouler were going to haunt him. Bouler had been convicted of possessing and selling

192

drugs a few years earlier and he was going to trial for, among other things, claiming a $57,000 check from Jordan was a loan rather than gambling winnings. I knew he had played with Bouler and, of course, wagered with Bouler because he had been a part of some of our games.

There was also the issue of photocopies of three more Jordan checks totaling $108,000 which were found in the trunk of a murdered bailbondsman's car.

This was all pretty ugly stuff for Mr. Corporate America.

Once the news on Slim and Company broke, my chances of collecting decreased. He had me overlaid on the Slim issue and I got thrown into the same category with all of his other golfing problems.

In truth, I was waiting for my name to come up in the press. I thought what we were wagering for might pop out, because Adolph knew it and Adolph had loose lips. Nothing ever came up, so Adolph must not have spilled anything.

When that stuff first surfaced, we were talking about the debt and I was listening to his pleas. I could and did empathize with his situation.

"It's too hot right now," he had said. "I can't handle dealing with it. Let me get through this temporary media problem."

That was his phrase. He saw it as a temporary media problem rather than a long-standing personal problem. That's what Stephenson meant when he talked about denial. That temporary media problem resurfaced in March of 1993 when that sleazebag newspaper, the National Enquirer, quoted Bouler as saying Jordan was addicted to gambling and golf. His problem was obviously bigger than I. I knew I wasn't his only "major" gambling adversary and I had no way of knowing if I was the biggest.

Back when all those reports first came out, I told him to take a couple months and work his way through it...but I did expect payment.

As we stood in the kitchen in Chicago, no payment had been

forthcoming. I was tired of excuses. I even told him maybe we could do an investment business deal *instead*. We both were in sports and entertainment and there was certainly some common ground of interest.

"My perception," I said, "is that you got caught with a couple of dirt bags and I don't want to be categorized with that element. The whole idea is insulting to me. You give me a check and it will be treated properly and booked properly."

I was trying to see if he *wouldn't* or *couldn't* pay. A token payment to move toward settlement would be a nice gesture.

"Rich," he said, "you've gotta give me time."

That was one of the few times he did not call me E-Man or Richard E.

By the time we left the kitchen, the basketball game was over.

I knew my friend was troubled, but at the time I knew no way to help him. He seemed to be A.O.K., at least in his mind.

———

The debt was at $902,000 after the very busy summer of 1992. He paid some and we played some. He got it down into six figures. I had given him more than one year to "work this thing out".

Michael Jordan was busy in 1992 because that was an Olympic year and he was an Olympian, the Dream Team's dreamboat attraction.

I was busy in 1992 because we were culminating the sale of the San Diego Sports Arena, which had been an ongoing project for what seemed like forever.

Our 1992 golf was a mini-binge compared to what we had done in the past. M.J. was in town with the Dream Team training at UC San Diego. We were able to get in three days of golf and that was it.

As I had previously stressed with Michael, we weren't doing any of that double or nothing stuff. We were playing for very big bucks, mind you, but the whole bankroll was not going to go on the line again.

Michael was due to arrive in San Diego in the latter part of June, not too long after he and the Bulls had finished off the Portland Trail Blazers for a second consecutive NBA championship. I was sitting at home late one night waiting for him to call and set our schedule and wondering what he had in mind about the debt.

My game was prepared. I had been hitting balls into the canyon to get ready for him. I thought my mind was prepared for the mental pressure of the golf matches as well as trying to close the transaction for that $1.25 million debt. The Sports Arena transaction seemed to be going sideways too, so I had many things on my mind.

I had no idea what he may have been thinking in terms of the debt. He had basically been dodging, denying and ignoring its existence. I didn't even know if he would be willing to talk about settling for less. My fear was that he might get angry and frustrated and possibly cause a confrontation. At one point, he had jokingly, I hoped, said he may as well shoot me as pay me $1.25 million. I wondered if maybe he really might be prone to violence. I didn't take it seriously.

I haven't hired a bodyguard or anything like that. For heaven's sake, M.J. is, or at least was, my friend. I hope he still is.

When he finally called, it turned out that the Olympic team's practice sessions were going to cut into our golf a bit. We would have three days to play, probably only 18 holes a day. To us, 18 holes was like foreplay without sex. He invited me to go to Barcelona, where the Olympics were being held, to play a few rounds of golf, but a family vacation and the Sports Arena business would not make that possible.

The conversation did raise my hopes that he was going to address the debt. He told me he would give me $50,000 when he arrived and another $50,000 every time I beat him, that being on top of whatever the wager might be that round. We would play for $100,000 each on match play and medal scores. He came to town $1.25 million down and me thinking the wildest of "chasing" was about to begin.

Our golf was scheduled for Tuesday, Wednesday and Thursday, June 23, 24 and 25, the first two days at Aviara up in the northern part of the county and the last day at the La Jolla Country Club.

M.J. told me we would be joined Tuesday by David Robinson and John Stockton from the Dream Team as well as a coach from Kansas. When he said a coach from Kansas, I thought he was talking about some golf coach or psychologist he had hired to help him with his game. It turned out to be Roy Williams, the basketball coach at the University of Kansas, a true joy as a conversationalist and golfing companion.

All my preparation certainly did not pay off during the Tuesday round at Aviara. If I had been a race horse, the chart would have said I faded in the stretch. I bogeyed 15 and 16, double-bogeyed 17 and bogeyed 18. My sand wedge even betrayed me, and that doesn't happen very often. He still only beat me one-up on the match bet and one-up on the medal bet, so I would have been in great shape if I hadn't fallen apart at the end. I put a $50,000 press on him on the 18th hole and my bogey was good enough to win the hole and bring my loss for the day down to $150,000. That brought the debt down to $1.1 million.

We didn't have much time for socializing, because I had to get back to San Diego for a concert by The Cure. M.J. did tell me his wife Juanita was mailing the $50,000 check he had promised.

I came back Wednesday to push the tab back to $1.25 million, shooting a 79 to Michael's 82. I was up the $200,000 on match and medal going to the 18th, where he did what I had done Tuesday. He threw a $50,000 press at me.

Neither one of us ended up in Position A off the tee on 18. He was in a fairway trap, maybe 210 yards from the hole and I had to take a drop from a water hazard on the right. Our next shots were fantastic. Michael hit a tremendous three-iron out of the trap and into the wind and onto the green.

"How's that, E-Man?" he said.

"Great out," I said.

We were always quick to congratulate each other when one of us would hit a special shot. We appreciated good golf, even when it was costing us.

I followed with a four-iron that hit the flag stick with a thunderous clang and whipped around the hole and away.

"How's that, Michael?" I said.

"Great recovery," M.J. said.

Unfortunately, my drop from the water cost me a stroke and my bogey lost to Michael's par. I picked up the $150,000 I had lost Tuesday.

"And remember, M.J.," I said, "you owe me another $50,000 because I beat you."

Juanita's check for $50,000 arrived and I stuck it in the bank before heading out to La Jolla for our round. Freddy Sarno, one of my regulars, and Barry Hippenstelle, a member, were joining us.

We were tied after nine holes, but I hit two shots out of bounds on No. 11 and that took the wind out of my sails. I ended up with a horrendous 85. M.J. was all over the place too. He had four or five birdies, which should have been harbingers of a great round, but he tossed in enough shanks to score a more modest 78. I would beat a 78 nine times out of 10, but this was that 10th time. He took me for $50,000 on a press too, so the day cost me $250,000.

The tab was now rounded off at $1 million in my favor, minus the $50,000 Juanita had sent. I later got another $50,000 check for the Wednesday round I had won and that brought M.J.'s debt to me down to exactly $902,000.

That was where it stayed for many more months.

Kerry and I had never discussed these numbers. She did not know how much I had risked. She did not know how much M.J. owed me.

She did not know where our innocent little games had taken us until she read the same black and white words you have been reading.

I could see the shock register on her face as she thumbed through the pages of the manuscript. She looked like she had been run over by a train and staggered to her feet with all her limbs in place.

"I never knew the dollar amount Richard lost to Michael or Michael lost to Richard," she told a friend, "until I saw it in print. Richard thought it was better not to tell me because I couldn't have dealt with it. It's so far removed from reality for me."

Remember, this was a woman with a Southern Baptist upbringing who had worked since she was 17. She learned the value of the dollar by working for every dollar she earned.

We had our joint household account, each of us contributing from our earnings, and we each had our mad money. She never knew exactly how mad I had gotten with my mad money.

"To gamble," she said, "is such a stupid thing. I knew he had gambled on the golf course and I knew he and Michael were exchanging bets. He would be up or down and that's all he would say. Rich has this superstition about not telling what he has won or what he has lost. I always felt that was Richard's money. It didn't affect what came into the house."

Thankfully, it never did affect what came into the house. I never wrote a check to Jordan off our joint account. When I wrote those three checks totaling $216,000, I wrote them on my account. If I had lost that money, I don't know how exactly I would have covered it. I do know I would have had to tell Kerry.

"We're awful damned lucky that the debt is in our behalf," Kerry told me when she read about that episode. "It scares the hell out of me that you could ever have been so out of control to let it get to that point. That really does frighten me. It upsets me just to think about it. It's just too weird."

Kerry was loving and concerned and probably relieved, at least that I had not come up the loser when so much was on the line. But she was truly and understandably frightened because this was a side of me she had not realized existed. Knowing that I gambled was bothersome enough, but she figured that was something I enjoyed and she just knew I would be sensible about it.

Talking again with a friend, she said: "It's such a dichotomy. Richard is the most grounded person I know. The man has not missed a meditation in 20 years...twice a day. You know how hard it is to be disciplined enough to do anything twice a day? And he has never missed his morning yoga either. I can tell you about him doing yoga in Gatwick Airport while we waited for a plane. He gets with Jordan and gets totally out of control. It's the weirdest thing. It's hard for me to understand."

One thing she never did was sit me down and demand that I never again play fast and loose on a golf course. She was not going to tell me what I could do or couldn't or should do or shouldn't. Needless to say, she was troubled by where I had been.

So was I.

We had a boxing card at the Sports Arena the Thursday night after we played La Jolla, but M.J. made me an offer I could not refuse. He invited me to Magic Johnson's hotel room in Torrey Pines for a card game with some guys from the Dream Team.

Obviously, this debt and our continuing dialogue about how it would be handled had not caused us to become estranged as friends. We had just played three days of golf and now I was invited to Magic's room to play cards with household names such as M.J., Clyde Drexler and Scottie Pippen. Jordan would not have allowed a hated and distrusted adversary into such elite company.

Some of the college guys who were like sparring partners for the Dream Team in practice were also there. I remember Michigan's Chris Webber, Duke's Bobby Hurley and North Carolina's Eric Montross. The college kids weren't in the card game because they didn't have the bucks to play with the big guys. The ante was $100 per hand and some of the pots got up to $3,000 and $4,000.

Magic and M.J. were poking fun at the poor impoverished collegians, and also poking fun at each other. Every time M.J. slid some cash into the pot, Magic would call it tennis shoe money. He got a kick out of razzing Jordan about his Nike contract.

Magic was a rather controversial member of the team because he had retired from the Lakers after announcing he was carrying the HIV virus. There was no needling about this subject at all. It was like verboten. The subject never came up, not even in a serious vein. However, I did notice some discomfort in the group when sexual conversations came up, as they tend to do when men are playing cards.

After awhile, a group of girls showed up all decked out like they were looking for a good time, if you know what I mean. Their breasts were spilling out or over their blouses and they were wearing tight skirts with hemlines which didn't seem too far below their waists. These were pretty girls who were definite distractions to the card players.

I knew two of the girls because they were regulars at our Sports Arena boxing events. Consequently, I got some special attention which caused a few raised eyebrows around the room. I was surprised to see the girls and I think they had to be a little surprised to see me. They had been to the boxing matches that night and one of them coquettishly said that she had missed me. I heard later from one of the girls that Magic was mildly irritated that I was getting more attention than he was.

Wives and girlfriends should be comforted, by the way, to know that no one paired off and nothing happened. It was just a flirtatious interlude in an evening of hard core card playing.

I left at about 1 a.m. and I left without about $4,000 I had lost to a bunch of guys who didn't really need it.

Later, when I was telling my buddy Bill Walton about it, he laughed.

"Rich," he said, "you work too hard for your money to be losing it to guys who have so much money it's like falling out of trees."

———

We had scheduled another 10 days of golf late in August of 1992, but it never came off. For one thing, I was busy with the arena. We have not played a round of golf since then, nor have we gotten together. That we haven't gotten together almost goes without saying, because we would have played golf if we had been as much as in the same area code.

We talked once about having a final hoopla at Augusta National and I had several dates lined up. We could have put more money on the line than the pros have ever seen at The Masters. It never came off because I could never pin Jordan down.

Michael's debt, thus, was still at $902,000, in spite of continuing negotiations through the mail and on the telephone. Through all my settlement discussions, I kept seeing and hearing a troubled Michael.

Contacting Jordan via the telephone is difficult. He is always changing numbers and I don't have the most recent. I do have the number to his answering machine, so I leave messages and ask him to call. I am at the mercy of his whims when it comes to actually calling. I have even sent requests via Federal Express that he give me a call, but it may as well be pony express as slowly as he responded.

My telephone rang on Nov. 12, 1992 and it was M.J.

"I'm sorry we didn't get to play much last summer," he said, "but my schedule was hectic. I'm looking forward to next summer."

We bantered back and forth about terms for upcoming matches. I underscored my point that we had gotten out of control and that future stakes should get back to reasonable levels. We had to play for something to make it interesting, but not for numbers which had obviously gone beyond his comfort zone as well as mine.

Naturally, I mentioned that $902,000.

"Don't worry, E-Man," he said. "I'll get a package out to you."

I went right back at him a day later with a letter detailing what I thought was a very reasonable proposal. I was trying to make my position clear and ease his mind about dealing with such a massive debt.

"You prefer to carry forward the full amount of $902,000 until June," I wrote. "I prefer to settle. We need a compromise and I'm willing to be overly accommodating. I will settle in full for one-third or $300,000. If you settle this week...Done! Done! Done! We can resolve this issue and get back to our normal games." I was trying to just put this behind me. How much more reasonable could I have been? I was giving away $600,000 I had very honestly won on the golf course. I was giving away $600,000 he had lost in spite of my protestations that it was ludicrous to raise our stakes to that level. Also consider that over 12 months had passed.

When we had been arguing about whether to go onward and upward with the stakes in 1991, Michael had made the point that $1.2 million was a manageable number to him.

"Are you prepared to pay $1.2 million?" I asked.

"E-Man," he said, "when you consider how much money I have, $1.2 million to me is like that $98,000 was to you."

It was probably a good argument, but it ended up having

one very large hole in it. He had seen my $98,000 check. He had seen that, plus another for the same amount. He had had my money in his hands. If he had beaten me that day, he would have had $196,000 of my money in the bank. That $1.2 million nibble out of his vast fortune, or at least $902,000 of it, had never made its way into my hands.

The package he had promised earlier in November had come disguised as an empty mail box.

Just before Thanksgiving, M.J. called again. He started talking about a professional football star who apparently owed him money from gambling losses on the golf course.

"I'm not bugging [him] for his money," Michael said, "so don't bug me for mine."

You can see where the conversation went from points I made in a letter I dashed off from my Ohio cabin before the family gathered for Thanksgiving dinner.

"After our conversation," I wrote, "I reflected on many of the things we talked about and I had the distinct impression you questioned my friendship because I was asking for payment. M.J., you have always said you would pay me. I believe you, I've given you time and I've offered you a steeply-discounted out so you can put this behind you. I've done this because I like you and believe you are a man of your word. Please do not confuse our friendship and your obligation to pay. The bottom line on friendship is that you should be able to ask for monies owed and you should be able to expect a friend to pay monies owed."

Our dialogue, written and spoken, was not going anywhere. I was confused and frustrated. I was asking a guy who had insisted he could play and pay at that level to fork over what he had lost. I was actually asking him to pay much less than he had lost. The whole issue was bigger than I had cared to make it, but the alternative was forgetting about it altogether. I couldn't do that.

I wrote him again on Feb. 8, 1993. This would be my last letter.

I made all the same points I had been making forever. I offered the same generous discount, which I am sure he never would have gotten from guys such as Slim. And I tried to separate myself from some of the riff-raff he had encountered in the past by enclosing my personal checking statement, which showed an average balance of $100,000. I reminded him that we had been in this cat and mouse game for 16 months. I told him our friendship had been taxed, but I hoped we could get this behind us and rekindle our friendship and golf once again at reasonable numbers. Obviously, I did insist some payment should be forthcoming. Principal was not a problem, but principle was. Through all this, I was worrying that I was pressuring him too much.

Voilà! My telephone rang the morning of March 8 and M.J. was on the line.

"Richard E," he said, "how are you doing?"

"Fine," I said. "How's that injured foot?"

"Getting better," he said.

He got to the point. At last, it seemed that I had gotten his attention.

I got your letter," he said. "I appreciate the discount to $300,000. I talked to my financial guy, Curtis Polk, and told him to call you about this situation. I'm sorry it's taken so long, but I'm really trying to hide this from my wife. All my financial stuff goes on a ledger, which I go over with her."

I could understand trying to keep it from Juanita. She probably thought that $50,000 check she mailed was the extent of the debt. I had not talked with Kerry about how much I had owed him or how much he currently owed me. It's kind of hard to explain being so stupid.

"I told my guy that you were quiet when all that other trouble came down and that we were tight and this was a gambling debt I wanted to take care of and get behind me," M.J. said. "I told him he could be confident talking with you and discussing how to handle it. The $300,000 is fine, but I'd like to spread it out a little bit, maybe $100,000 now and another $100,000 a couple of months down the road."

Curtis Polk called me and I thought it was worked out.

Nothing happened until late March, when a cashier's check for $100,000 arrived. It was written on the American National Bank and Trust Company of Chicago and payable to Richard Esquinas. It was check number 1431650, to be precise.

Nothing in the packet suggested Jordan's involvement. I could see where he would be a little gun-shy about signing personal checks after the Slim business. And maybe this was a way he could keep it from Juanita.

It arrived Federal Express with a cover letter written by Wayne A. McCoy on the letterhead of Schiff, Hardin & Waite, described as a partnership including professional corporations. Maybe M.J. is one of those corporations.

"Dear Mr. Esquinas," McCoy wrote. "In furtherance of assisting our client in consummating his arrangements with you, I am enclosing a cashier's check in the amount of $100,000 payable to your order. Thank you for the prompt return of your notarized affidavit confirming the necessary representations."

The affidavit was a mere confirmation that I had received a package from the client, nothing like an acknowledgement of payment in full. It was nothing contractual at all, more like the reception of a certified letter and statement that I would declare the amount as taxable income.

One thing you can say about M.J. is that he is a tough negotiator. The payment had taken his debt down from $300,000 to $200,000 rather than from $902,000 to $802,000. It also shows how understanding and reasonable I have been. Another payment is scheduled for June 1, 1993 and then January 1994. I was well into writing this book and had been advised not to mention the book to M.J. for fear of conversations heating up to where "extortion" type language would come up.

Michael Jordan's situation is and has been of tremendous concern to me. It's much more than the fact that he owes me money. It's the insanity which was pre-destined to cause one of us to owe an incredible amount of money to the other, and it could well have been me. I also have concern for M.J. personally, both in terms of his gambling and in the terms of potential personal ramifications.

My mind has churned for months with two basic questions regarding this debt:

1. Won't M.J. pay?

Or...

2. Can't M.J. pay?

Regardless of pay, I knew M.J. was troubled, and this concerned me. If he simply won't pay, I am very disappointed in him. I thought there was more to our friendship, more to the honor and sincerity of our games. Over all those months of all those summers and all those hours we shared on golf courses, we played the game at its highest level of integrity. We never fudged on the rules of this most gentlemanly of games, excepting, of course, our occasional reciprocal mulligans on the first tee.

It would absolutely blow my mind that so honorable a relationship could be so tainted by one party failing to honor a debt incurred in those matches.

It is totally incongruous with the nature of what we were all about as friends and adversaries.

But what if Michael Jordan simply cannot pay? What if his financial world has gone sideways for one reason or another? What if all those untold millions he makes annually from basketball and endorsements has not been enough to sustain him?

That is a frightening thought. Michael has far too much pride to come to me and tell me he simply cannot afford to pay. It would be hard to imagine that that could possibly be the case.

Unless...

What if this gambling loss incurred to me is just one of many?

We already know there are others out there, but we don't know how many. Michael could have a very serious gambling problem and it does not take too long for dollars to add up at his preferred levels of wagering. I continually worried about M.J.'s mental health, his mindset, his managing of stress, etc.

I first went into therapy a mere two months after those crazy rounds we played in September in 1991. I was concerned for myself much more so than for M.J. I assumed he was staying within his means, but I knew I hadn't.

In retrospect, I wonder if maybe my concern wasn't misplaced.

I don't really think I am a compulsive and addicted gambler in a classic sense.

My therapist disagrees with me, of course, but I largely confine myself to gambling on the golf course, where I am not at home without some dollars on the line. I play a little black jack in Las Vegas, but I don't beat a path back-and-forth from San Diego to chase losses or look for the big hit. I make my annual Super Bowl bet, but never play football on a week-to-week basis. That doesn't sound out of control to me.

My one and only totally out of control experience has been gambling against M.J. on the golf course. I submit that I could only have gotten out of control with a Michael Jordan, because he was what might be called a trophy opponent. Teeing it up against such a famed adversary piqued my competitive juices and drove me over the edge.

Michael Jordan found in me a worthy opponent, both from a financial and competitive point of view. I also happened to be a pillar in a very large community, which made me a safe person to engage in terms of respectability. Given the reports which have already surfaced about gambling bets he incurred elsewhere, I fear he was not always so discriminating in the making of his games.

In M.J.'s quest for the euphoric experience, the mood-altering rush of a high stakes game, I have this fear that he might have gotten into games and opponents he could not handle.

I wonder if he has much more of a problem with gambling than I do.

Would he admit this? He hasn't yet.

However, I assure you that his family, friends and advisers are aware of his problem. If they cannot see it, it would have to be because they are blind. In truth, they are blind, but only because they care not to see...or admit what they are seeing. Hey, this is not a fun situation. As Adolph would have said, M.J. is their horse. They ride him. He allows it because they provide him the insulation of a comfort zone and part of that insulation is the isolation from reality. Maybe it is possible they cannot see it or don't understand it.

It's a given that M.J. gambles. Chicago *Tribune* sportswriter Sam Smith wrote very matter-of-factly about it in his book "The Jordan Rules." He reported that Jordan went to Atlantic City after a 1990 playoff game in Philadelphia and was seen at a craps table playing with $500 chips. Smith wrote that M.J. drove straight from there to the Bulls' practice the next morning.

A lot of people do such things, but isn't there a little cause for alarm when a basketball star does it in the midst of a playoff series?

When Curtis Polk called, I had the audacity to raise the issue of M.J.'s gambling.

"How well do you know Michael?" he said.

"Pretty well," I said. "We went through four summers of mucho golf."

"Well," he said, "M.J. is a little hard-headed about that subject."

He was hard-headed alright. Gambling may be the most deniable of addictions, because it has no outward physical manifestation. If M.J.'s problem was alcohol or drugs, for example, he could not walk into the locker room or, for that matter, living room and hide it.

Instead, compulsive gambling is a cancer that eats away at the wallet. Most people so afflicted will not seek help until they have tapped family and friends for all the resources they need to finance the big hit that will bail them out. They may not seek help until they are hopelessly in debt and their families and their homes are gone as well.

Michael Jordan is not at that point, obviously. I'm not exactly sure where he is, but he is traveling hard and fast on a very dangerous road.

Who should tell him? In a unique verbal and non-verbal way, he seemed to be asking me for help. I've seen him like few have, but what to do with that awareness troubles me. I've looked him eye to eye and seen his illness, heard it in his voice...like only his long time friend and opponent could.

"Michael," I have frequently said, "are you alright? Do you need some help?"

When I say frequently, I mean virtually every time we talked over the past 18 months.

"Naw," he would always answer. "I'm OK, E-Man."

I have tried to get through to him, to no avail. I can hardly get two words into the subject. At this point, I really can't get to him for a conversation on any subject, much less on so profound a concern for his welfare.

Michael is so stubborn it may take a sledge-hammer to get through to him.

Maybe, in my own way, I can be the sledge-hammer. Hopefully his family, friends, teammates, business partners, and fans will put their arms around him, be accepting and help him. And hopefully Michael will go inward like I have to wrestle with the gross realities of out of control gambling. The realities we shared.

EPILOGUE

Through my individual therapy, self- reflection, reading and attendance at Gamblers' Anonymous meetings, I have learned a great deal about the problem gambling has become for millions of people around the world.

I am one who has that problem and I fear Michael Jordan does as well.

I have put together a list, from a layman's perspective obviously, of solutions I would suggest for anyone who has the problem or has a loved one or friend who has the problem.

1. Get involved with Gamblers Anonymous! Look in the phone book and call the number of Gamblers Anonymous to find out where the closest meeting is to you and attend as many as you can. They are free and they have a proven track record of helping thousands of compulsive gamblers to stop gambling. (If you can't find their number call (213) 386-8789 for information on your closest meeting).

2. Get into individual therapy with a therapist, who has experience working with compulsive gamblers. The insight given and changes you will make are well worth the money invested.

3. If you are related to a compulsive gambler, get involved with Gam-Anon. Find out where the meeting nearest you is and attend. It can really help give you an understanding of the compulsive gambler's problem and what you can and can't do about it.

4. Don't be afraid to confront friends or loved ones whom you strongly suspect have gambling problems. Consider doing an *intervention*, when a group of family members and/or close friends confront the gambler to recognize the problem and get help.

5. Do not enable compulsive gamblers. By lending them money to get out of their messes. And don't look the other way and pretend like they don't have a problem.

6. Join and contribute to non-profit organizations such as the California Council on Compulsive Gambling (408-TRY-9099) and the National Council on Compulsive Gambling (212-765-3833).

7. Lobby and write letters to your local, state and federal politicians and advise them of your opposition to increasing the spread of legalized gambling. Protest government involvement in the gambling business, such as state lotteries. Push for laws to keep gambling from becoming a "living room" activity through television or computer access.

8. Lobby and donate money or help allocate tax money to help increase funding for research on compulsive gambling and its effect on people as well as prevention and treatment.

9. Read Gamblers Anonymous literature, books and magazine articles on compulsive gambling to learn more about the nature of this problem and what you can do about it.

10. And most *importantly*, remember to take life one day at a time.

Bibliography

The following list of publications was used in researching and writing this book:

Robert McClory, "The Lure of Gambling's Easy Money," *Utne Reader*, September-October, 1992.

Chris Welles, "America's Gambling Fever," *Business Week*, April 24, 1989.

John Bradshaw, *Bradshaw On: The Family*, Health Communications Inc., 1988.

Multiple authors, "Gambling," *Sports Illustrated*, March, 1986.

Clive Gammon, "Tales of Self-Destruction," *Sports Illustrated*, March, 1986.

Jim Naughton, *Taking To The Air*, Warner Books, 1992.

Sam Smith, *The Jordan Rules*, Simon & Schuster, 1992.

Bob Greene, *Hang Time*, Doubleday, 1992.

Richard J. Rosenthal, M.D., "Pathological Gambling," *Psychiatric Annals*, February, 1992.

Richard Demek, "The Investigation: Did the NBA Really Probe Michael Jordan's Activities?", *Sports Illustrated*, April, 1992.

George J. Church, "Why Pick on Pete?", *Time Magazine*, July, 1989.